TERRORISM

THE BASICS

'A concise and very accessible introduction to terrorism, touching on all the major debates and issues. Ideal for those who need a quick introduction to the area and a good choice for students coming at the subject for the first time.'

Professor Andrew Silke, *Director Terrorism Studies, University of East London, UK*

Terrorism: The Basics is the perfect introduction for anyone interested in one of the most discussed, written about and analysed aspects of modern life. Common misconceptions about the nature of terrorism and terrorists themselves are dispelled as the authors provide clear and jargon-free answers to the big questions:

- What does terrorism involve?
- Who can be classified as a terrorist?
- What are terrorists trying to achieve?
- Who are the supporters of terrorism?
- Can there ever be an end to terrorist activity?

These questions and more are answered with reference to contemporary groups and situations allowing readers to relate the theory to what is broadcast in the news. Written with clarity and insight, this book is the perfect first book on terrorism for students of all levels.

James Lutz is a Professor of Political Science at Indiana University-Purdue University, USA and **Brenda Lutz** received her Ph.D in Politics from the University of Dundee, Scotland. They have collaborated on a great number of works dealing with terrorism including major textbooks, edited collections.

The Basics

TERRORISM
THE BASICS

James Lutz and Brenda Lutz

LONDON AND NEW YORK

First published 2011
by Routledge

2 Park Square, Milton Park, Abingdon, Oxon, OX14 4RN
Simultaneously published in the USA and Canada
by Routledge
711 Third Avenue, New York, NY 10017

Routledge is an imprint of the Taylor & Francis Group, an informa business

Typeset in Aldus by
HWA Text and Data Management, London
Printed and bound in Great Britain by
TJ International Ltd, Padstow, Cornwall

British Library Cataloguing in Publication Data
A catalogue record for this book is available from the British Library

Library of Congress Cataloging in Publication Data
Lutz, James M.
 Terrorism : the basics / James Lutz and Brenda Lutz.
  p. cm.
 Includes bibliographical references.
 1. Terrorism – United States. 2. Terrorism – United States – Prevention.
 3. Terrorism – Government policy – United States. 4. National security –
 United States. 5. Terrorists – United States. 6. Terrorism. I. Lutz, Brenda J.,
 1957– II. Title.
 HV6432.L895 2011
 363.325–dc22   2010034125

ISBN: 978-0-415-57333-7 (hbk)
ISBN: 978-0-415-57334-4 (pbk)
ISBN: 978-0-203-83198-4 (ebk)

To our beautiful daughters

Carol and Tessa

and

our loyal St. Bernards, Annie, Clarabelle, Oliver
and Barnaby

CONTENTS

ACKNOWLEDGEMENTS

The authors owe a great deal too many people, including, of course the academics who have provided important studies of terrorism for us to draw upon. We would like to thank students and colleagues who provided questions, ideas, and concepts throughout the years that we have been writing about and teaching about terrorism. These contributions have been incorporated into the pages that follow. We would also like to thank the individuals at Routledge who have worked on this project and who have made it possible, especially Andy Humphries, Sophie Thomson, and Rebecca Shillabeer. Andy Humphries initially suggested the project, and everyone else at Routledge has been very supportive. Notwithstanding all the assistance that we have received, we remain responsible for any errors of omission or commission.

Of course, as with everything we undertake our daughters provide the motivation for all of our endeavors. The encouragement we receive from our daughter Carol keeps us focused on our work. Our daughter, Tessa, inspires us each day. When all is said and done they are the reason why we write.

PREFACE

When we first started writing and research on terrorism in 1998, we were concerned that too much attention was focused on terrorism in the Middle East. It appeared that many writers have already forgotten about the Red Brigades, the Baader-Meinhof Gang, and similar groups in Western Europe and Latin America. As we continued researching in this area, the focus on the Middle East increased after the attacks of 9/11 on New York City and Washington, DC. Now, quite naturally, the focus has been on Al Qaeda and other Islamic terrorists. Much has been written, some good and some not so good, on the subject of Islamic terrorism. What has sometimes been lost in the discussion is the fact that terrorism involves more than Islamic groups and more than the Middle East.

Our contribution to the Routledge basics series is designed to provide information on the underlying issues involved in terrorism and to help place Islamic political violence within the broader perspective of global terrorism. There are other groups that have engaged in terrorism, and these organizations will be discussed. This book will provide the essential basic information on terrorism. It will also present an appropriate context for understanding global terrorism today and in the future.

Of course, this book is just a starting point for understanding terrorism and the context in which it occurs. Further, it is designed to provide the reader with a basic framework and basic knowledge of the subject. Given the volume of material that now exists, anyone interested in a deeper understanding of terrorism can find materials on their own (starting with bibliography in this book and the suggested readings which have their own bibliographies and references). This book, however, should provide the necessary starting point for exploring the topic in more depth.

WHAT IS TERRORISM?

Concern over terrorism has become a part of life in the twenty-first century. Although terrorism is not new, the events of **9/11**/2001 in the United States, the **Madrid train bombings** in 2004, the **London transport bombings** in 2005, continuing suicide attacks in Iraq and Israel/Palestine, and terrorist violence in many other places has focused attention on these types of events. Terrorism, of course, has occurred in many countries and in many contexts. It is not new phenomenon even though events such as these have made terrorism a more prominent concern in many countries. As a result, it is very important to have a better understanding of what terrorism is – why it occurs, who is responsible, what the terrorists hope to accomplish, and what the future holds for terrorism. These questions and others are basic to the topic of this book.

Although many people have a good idea of what terrorism is, it is useful from the outset to have a working definition as to what can be considered terrorism (and what cannot be considered terrorism). It has frequently been stated that: "One person's freedom fighter is another person's terrorist." Basically this statement says that terrorism, like beauty, is in the eye of the beholder. People have a tendency to brand those who use violence for purposes that they disagree with as terrorists while they regard those using the same kinds of violence in a "just cause" as freedom fighters. It is essential to have a definition that will apply to violent activities regardless of who is opposing or supporting the individuals involved or who the targets are. The fact that terrorism includes all kinds of groups should not blind us to the fact that what might be defined as terrorism by virtually everyone, could be acceptable to others in some circumstances. If Jews in Europe facing Hitler's efforts to exterminate them had resorted to terrorism in self-defense, such actions would clearly have been justifiable.

DEFINITION OF TERRORISM

There are many definitions of terrorism that have been used. Oftentimes the definitions are created to identify certain groups as falling within the definition since the term terrorist has a very negative association. If a group is labeled as a terrorist group, then it is easier to mobilize public opinion against it. If supporters of the group are considered to be freedom fighters or a national liberation front, the likelihood that they will be able to generate more sympathy is increased. Other definitions attempt to be more neutral, but it is important to recognize that any definition will include groups that some individuals would exclude because they agree with the goals of the organizations. In other cases, the definition might exclude groups that others think should be considered as terrorists. The best approach, of course, is to first specify a definition and then to determine whether or not a particular group fits the definition. Even with the arguments over the definitions, there are some common elements used by scholars, governments, and journalists.

There are a number of basic components necessary in order for a group to be considered as a terrorist organization. The following characteristics combine to provide a useful and usable definition of terrorism.

> Terrorism involves political aims and motives. It is violent or threatens violence. It is designed to generate fear in a target audience that extends beyond the immediate victims of the violence. The violence is conducted by an identifiable organization. The violence involves a non-state actor or actors as either the perpetrator, the victim of the violence, or both. Finally, the acts of violence are designed to create power in situations in which power previously had been lacking (i.e. the violence attempts to enhance the power base of the organization undertaking the actions).

The key elements of the definition will be discussed in the sections to follow. The importance of the various characteristics will be obvious in many of the other chapters as well. This definition will underlay much of the discussion in the following chapters and will demonstrate why it is important and why it combines in a useful way to describe the phenomenon that we know as terrorism.

POLITICAL OBJECTIVES

The first key element of this definition is that the violence is primarily undertaken for political reasons. The fact that the actions are initiated to achieve political ends is a key element that separates terrorist acts from other forms of violence. The political objectives separate terrorism from violence that is launched for financial reasons or because of personal issues. Kidnappings of prominent political leaders or corporate executives to make political statements are different from those kidnappings that serve as criminal ventures to raise money for the abductors. The use of fear to extort money from businesses (the protection rackets of American gangster fame) is criminal, not political. Sometimes, of course, opposition groups have used kidnapping or bank robberies to finance their organizations, and they have been known to use violence or the threat of violence to levy "revolutionary taxes" on groups that could be forced to pay. In these cases, the goals are still generally political because the money received is used to fund subsequent political activities, including possibly more violence, rather than leading to gains in personal wealth.

While political objectives are a key for defining terrorism, the goals that are sought by terrorists can fall into a number of categories. The terrorists may be seeking to have a change in policies, or a change in leadership, or even a change in boundaries. The attainment of these objectives may be ones that are seen by the terrorists to be immediately possible or they may see them as being the end points of a long struggle. Some groups have indeed geared themselves for a long struggle to achieve these goals while others may believe that a show of violence is all that is necessary to topple the government in power or bring about the other changes that they desire.

VIOLENCE

The second element of a terrorist action is that the activity involves violence or the threat of violence. Requests for changes, demonstrations, and petitions are not terrorism, no matter how disconcerting they may be to a government. Although massive demonstrations may make a government apprehensive about the future, there is no direct threat of violence. Actual violence is fairly obvious when it occurs. Terrorism can also involve the credible threat of violence. One situation in which the threat of violence might be present would be one in which a group issues an ultimatum requiring action; if the appropriate action does not occur, violence will result. The threat of violence is only likely to be effective as a technique, however, with a group that has already demonstrated that it is able and willing to use violence. A political organization that has never undertaken any type of political violence is unlikely to be credible in its threats. Once violence has been used, however, the threat of additional violence may generate the necessary fear that the dissident group desires and lead the government to give in to the specific demands of the group. Hoaxes can, as a consequence, be part of a terrorist campaign, especially when they follow upon actual earlier violent actions.

TARGET AUDIENCE

For violence, and even political violence, to qualify as terrorism, it must include a target audience beyond the immediate victims. The violence is intended to influence the target audience or audiences as part of the attempt to gain the political objectives of the organization. If a political leader is assassinated with the goal of removing that individual in order to permit the next in line to move up, the death is political violence, but it has no target audience and it is not terrorism. It is a practical effort to put someone else in power. For an assassination to be a terrorist action, it must involve parties beyond the assassin or assassins and the immediate victim. If a political leader is assassinated in order to send a message to other members of the political elite that they need to change policies or make concessions in order to avoid a similar fate, then that assassination is a terrorist act. Bombings of buildings (with or without casualties) or car bombs in crowded areas are often intended to show the general public that they are vulnerable. The resulting fear may lead the public to put pressure on the government to change policies or weaken public support for the leaders in power who clearly are unable to protect the citizens from dissidents. Frequently the victims of terrorist actions are members of the target audience since that is the easiest way to send a message to all the other members of the target audience. One of the primary goals of the violence is to create fear in the target audience. Thus, the immediate victims are usually not chosen specifically, but are simply convenient targets. The target audience, not the immediate victims of a terrorist act, is the key group that terrorist organizations are attempting to influence, and the goal is to generate fear in the target audience.

The need to reach a target audience is one reason why terrorist groups seek publicity. If no one knows of a terrorist act, the goals have not been achieved. If the deaths of government personnel are ascribed to a plane crash rather than a bomb on the aircraft, the target audience will draw the wrong conclusion about threats to the state or to the safety of individuals. The need for publicity is a key reason why some terrorist organizations have established pre-set code words with the media so that they can authenticate the claims of the organization when they provide a warning that a bomb is about to detonate. Of course, it will not be necessary in all cases for particular organizations to claim credit for particular terrorist actions. If a terrorist group has been active in the past, violence against the government or its supporters will be ascribed to the group without any need for a pronouncement from the terrorist group. The local situation and the target will often make it clear that the cause of a particular group of dissidents is behind the activity. If swastikas are painted on a Jewish synagogue, the anti-Semitic message is obvious. If a car bomb goes off at the headquarters of the ruling party, the general population is likely to know whether it is a local minority group or whether it is the political opposition that is behind the attack. Even if the source of the violence is obvious, it will still be necessary for information about the action to reach the target audience.

ORGANIZATION

For political violence to be terrorism there must be an identifiable organization. A lone individual is unlikely to be able to carry out the actions, reach the target audience, and present the political demands for the changes that are necessary to end the violence. An effective campaign to create change also requires enough actions to be credible, an effort beyond a single individual over time. A political assassination to change a leader can be very effective even if the assassin is killed *if the change in leadership results in a desired change in the government.* If the leader is simply replaced by another person with the same program and policies, then nothing has been accomplished and the solitary individual who was seeking the change is likely to be killed or captured. Terrorist actions almost inevitably lead to casualties or arrests among the dissidents; thus, a single individual is very likely to be captured or killed. Large organizations do not have to be as concerned about casualties among the members, while smaller organizations have to conserve scarce resources (members).

Theodore Kaczynski, the **Unabomber** in the United States, is a classic example of the limitations inherent with campaigns by one individual. Kaczynski sent package bombs to a variety of individuals. He was essentially upset over the pace of modernization and damaging changes that were occurring in the environment. His bombings over the years inspired fear, but the target audience was unclear, and it was not obvious what actions the target audience was expected to take. The FBI and other police agencies knew that the bombings were related due to forensic analyses, but they were unable to establish the linkages between the victims, and were they were unable to identify the political agenda of the person behind them. Until Kaczynski had a rambling manifesto published, his goals were unclear. Once they were published, he was identified by his writing and arrested. His activities demonstrate the need for a broader organization and the need for publicity (as well as the dangers that may come with greater publicity).

Organizational structures have changed in recent times with improved communications and transportation that have resulted in a smaller world. Organizations, such as **Al Qaeda**, can maintain linkages with each other and even support or cooperate with groups that are not a formal part of the organization. Al Qaeda, for example, has supported actions by other groups that were not part of the organization. It provided funding and technical support for a number of attacks when it agreed with the goals and when it thought there was a chance of successful actions. With mobile phones, the internet, and other forms of communication, such improvised or informal cooperative arrangements can extend the reach of a formal organization and make it much more dangerous. Basically terrorist groups set up a network operation. The network does increase the dangers and at the same time often makes it more difficult for the authorities to infiltrate informers or breakup the groups involved.

Another form of organization that is present in the modern world is what has come to be called **leaderless resistance**. Leaderless resistance involves individuals or small groups that identify with some larger cause acting to achieve the goals of a larger group. There may be an organization that provides some direction to those wishing to undertake such "lone wolf" attacks by indicating appropriate targets or disseminating information on how to make bombs or use other types of violence. The individuals who were responsible for the London transport bombings in 2005 were not formal members of Al Qaeda or any other formal group. They did identify, however, with the goals of Al Qaeda and similar groups, and they saw their action as part of the broader struggle of militant Islam against activities of the West with which they disagreed. These individual attacks do add to the strength of a group, and there is an element of implied organization present. There has to be some group that provides a central reference for the identification and perhaps even to provide information on targets and techniques. The individuals agree with the broader goals, and they clearly seek to link themselves with the broader cause and to influence a target audience. This kind of loosely coordinated activity thus exists in addition to the more conventionally organized groups; they do not replace them completely.

The **anarchists** were a group that operated in the late 1800s and the early 1900s seeking to change political systems to provide greater benefits for average citizens and the working class. The anarchists first attempted to bring about political change through education efforts designed to convince the political elite to extend greater rights and freedom to the general population. When these efforts failed, the anarchists decided to use violence in their attempts to bring about change. The anarchists attacked political leaders in many countries. The targets included reigning monarchs and elected political leaders. Some were members of organized groups, but in some cases individual anarchists would attempt to assassinate prominent leaders as part of this broader struggle. The anarchists thus provide one of the earlier examples of a form of leaderless resistance.

ACTORS OTHER THAN STATES INVOLVED

The actions of countries directed against other countries are excluded in this definition of terrorism. Countries involved in wars have always attempted to inspire terror in their enemies, but these kinds of activities are part of international relations. Similarly, in situations of tension between countries, their intelligence agencies may engage in activities designed to spread fear or undermine their opponents. The **CIA** (American Central Intelligence Agency) and allies like **Secret Intelligence Service** (United Kingdom) as well as the **KGB** (former Soviet intelligence service) engaged in many kinds of activities designed to weaken the Soviet Union and its allies or the United States and its allies respectively during the Cold War between these countries. At least, at times, the activities of these agencies were successful. The exclusion of activities between states is not intended to dismiss the importance of their actions, nor is it intended to deny that sometimes these activities can be horrific and cause devastation. During World War II, for example, both sides bombed cities in an effort to destroy the morale of the civilian populations. The bombings culminated with the destruction of Dresden and the dropping of atomic bombs on Hiroshima and Nagasaki, all of which resulted in the deaths of large numbers of people. Massacres of civilians and similar types of activities undertaken by government forces during wartime are clearly evil as well. Actions such as these are not being dismissed and definitely not accepted. They are simply part of another area of study and analysis for political science and international relations.

There are three situations in which terrorism can occur within this definition: first, dissidents may target a government or governments; second, governments may target a group of their own citizens or support groups that target a group of their own citizens; or third, groups may target each other with such violence independent of government. By far the most frequent form that terrorism has taken is violence by dissident groups against their own government or foreign governments. The groups involved are using the violence as part of an effort to get the government to change policies or to bring about other changes in a political system. Governments may also tolerate situations in which local groups use violence in an effort to create terror in some portion of its own population that it fears or distrusts. Since governments have police, security, and military forces to deal with what are perceived to be domestic threats, this form of terrorism is less likely to occur. If the targets of the violence are groups opposed to the government, there may even be active support from the authorities. Finally, groups may battle among themselves in efforts to end the political activities of the opposing group or drive out another group. In Turkey in the 1970s left-wing groups and right-wing groups targeted each other with violence and terrorism as they competed to bring about different types of changes. When India and Pakistan were being formed out of the former British India in 1947, Hindus and Muslims attacked each other, and Muslim refugees from India and Hindu refugees from the new state of Pakistan fled in fear.

WEAPON OF THE WEAK

The last part of the definition depends on the fact that terrorist actions are used to improve the power situation of the organization that is using this form of political violence. While the specific agendas of groups using terrorism are quite different, they all share this characteristic. They are attempting to improve their power situation – to increase their probability of being able to influence political decisions. Terrorist campaigns are frequently mounted by organizations that have failed to bring about their desired changes by other means, i.e. they are politically weak. The groups have failed in democratic elections to gain enough power to bring about change. Governments have ignored peaceful protests and appeals, or they have been met by government repression that prevents further efforts at peaceful change.

A group that can influence the military to undertake a coup in their country to take over the government to bring about the changes that are desired will not have to rely on terrorism. Groups in the past that could organize a rebellion and mobilize sufficient troops to march on the capital and attempt to defeat the government did not have to rely on terrorism since they have more powerful sources. When civil wars break out, both sides have sufficient forces to engage in such a conflict. While one or both sides in a civil war may rely on terror techniques much as countries do during wartime, these activities are not central to the conflict. Terrorism remains a tool to be used by groups that lack the possibility of these kinds of peaceful or violent protests against a current government. Since they are relatively powerless in the conventional political setting of their own society due to limited electoral appeal or limited support in the face of government repression, they resort to unconventional means (terrorism) in an effort to improve their power base. When governments turn to supporting terrorist groups against their own citizens it is because they cannot be sure that they will be successful in relying on conventional police techniques or forms of repression. Thus, their reliance on terrorism is also a reflection of weakness.

ATTACKING CIVILIANS

Some definitions of terrorism include the specification that the targets of terrorist violence are civilians. The insurgent attacks on military personnel in Iraq, for example, are not normally considered terrorist attacks. Civilians are often the targets for terrorism because the target population consists mainly of civilians and terrorists usually attack members of the target audience. Adding this component to a definition of terrorism, however, adds complexity. Are off-duty police, reserve military personnel, or civilians acceptable targets? What about civilian employees working on military bases? When attacks result in the deaths of both civilians and military personnel, are the civilians considered the targets or acceptable collateral damage? To include this component in the definition also may require knowledge of the intentions of those launching the attacks. As a consequence, it does not seem necessary to include the targeting of civilians as a key component of the definition, but it is useful to recognize that civilian populations are often the intended targets of terrorist attacks, if for no other reason than to increase the resulting fear among a target population as noted.

TERRORISM AS PSYCHOLOGICAL WARFARE

Terrorism is ultimately a form of psychological warfare. The goal of the terrorist group is to spread fear in the target population in order to bring about some kind of change. The goals of the terrorists have been met when the greatest amount of fear has been caused by the terrorist attack. The most effective terrorist actions are those that reach the largest number of people. The attacks on the World Trade Center and the Pentagon on September 11, 2001 in the United States generated immense amounts of fear because of the death toll and the symbolism involved. The 2005 transport bombings in London did not kill as many people but indicated to many in the United Kingdom that they could be at risk. The **anthrax** scare in the United States coming so soon after the attacks of 9/11 in October of 2001 generated a great deal of fear while resulting in the deaths of less than a dozen people. The hope of the terrorists is that the attacks will undermine confidence in the public or the elite and lead to the desired changes or to the weakening of a state, which in turn makes it more vulnerable to continued terrorism or other forms of violence.

One of the things that can heighten the fear that occurs with terrorism is the idea that the violence is random. In actuality, terrorism is seldom random by intent; in fact, it has to be distinctly

Fear in a target audience is one of the key goals of campaigns of terrorism. Terrorism is ultimately a form of psychological warfare that is directed against this target audience. (Wilkinson 1975: 81)

non-random in order to be successful. The targets of terrorist attacks, whether they are people or objects, are chosen from among a similar group of targets. One member of the group is interchangeable with another. The randomness occurs in the sense that any individual member of a group can become the target for the violence to send the message to others. While the victims of a lethal attack are likely to be random in the sense of being victims, they become victims because they are members of a specific group. The appearance of complete randomness in the choice of targets, however, can increase the fear of the target audience. The end result of this situation for the target audience is the knowledge that any of them could indeed become victims and that no one is safe.

DIPLOMATIC AND LEGAL DEFINITIONS OF TERRORISM

The definition used above is one that is designed to aid in understanding terrorism, but it cannot serve as an appropriate definition in a court of law. Governments usually need a more precise legal definition if they are going to use their courts and legal systems to try, convict, and punish individuals who are involved in terrorist actions, and it may be essential for a government that has to decide whether or not a person accused of terrorism elsewhere should be extradited. In many cases, however, national legal systems will not require any special definition of terrorism. Hijacking an airplane, setting off a bomb, and killing people are already crimes under national laws, even when the crimes are undertaken for political purposes. If a state wishes to impose stiffer penalties for crimes associated with terrorism, however, then some sort of legal definition becomes important. Prosecutors must be able to prove that political intent or political objectives were behind the violence. Sometimes terrorists on trial are more than happy to proclaim their political goals, but in other cases such intent may be quite difficult to prove. A legal definition does not require the specification of a target audience or information on the level of organization involved. Similarly, if a national legislature desires to prohibit financial contributions to terrorist groups, then the government has to provide some system for designating which groups are prohibited and how they are defined. That type of legal definition may be more difficult.

Efforts at the international level to come up with treaties and conventions banning terrorism have, to date, not been particularly successful. One of the problems with such a convention is the difficulty in defining terrorism in terms that would be acceptable to all the countries concerned. Some countries, especially in the developing world, are afraid that national liberation fronts would be considered terrorist groups. Arab countries have long considered Palestinian groups opposed to Israel to be national liberation movements rather than terrorist groups, and they would resist any international definition that would automatically consider these groups to be terrorist organizations. As Andrew Silke (2004: 5) noted, even close allies can disagree about the definition of terrorism. Early in the twenty-first century both the United States and the United Kingdom had lists of organizations that they considered to be terrorist groups. Thirteen different dissident groups were on both lists, but the United Kingdom had eight groups not on the US list, and the United States had fifteen not on the British list.

Countries would find it inconvenient to extradite or prosecute persons who would be considered as terrorists under an international convention. The United States or United Kingdom would have been loath to extradite Iraqi dissidents responsible for bombs directed against the regime of Saddam Hussein when he was still in power. Governments no doubt prefer a certain amount of flexibility in determining who constitutes a terrorist, permitting the government to take whatever actions seem best. Governments will at times have to make the distinction between freedom fighter and terrorist – when the same action is acceptable and when it is not. Politicians will have to decide, and national public opinion will be important in that decision. Governments will always be caught between choosing to support consistent approaches and taking into account special circumstances that might exist.

GUERRILLA WARFARE AND TERRORISM

Terrorism and guerrilla warfare have some things in common. Both are weapons of the weak used by dissident groups that lack the ability to challenge the government in other ways. Guerrilla groups, however, generally target police, the security forces, and the military. They are less likely to target civilians in their attacks. When guerrilla groups begin to target civilians, they usually cross over into terrorism, and some dissident groups may indeed combine military action against military forces and terror attacks against soft civilian targets. Effective guerrilla warfare may require more resources and personnel than terrorism; thus, a shift to guerrilla tactics from purely terrorist attacks may signal the success of the dissident movement in moving to a higher stage. While guerrilla tactics may be used by dissident movements, they are unlikely to be used by governments to attacks their own citizens. Governments are more likely to rely on repression not terrorism.

CONCLUSIONS

While there are many definitions of terrorism, the keys include political objectives, violence, target audiences, organization, a non-state actor as the target or perpetrator, and groups that have limited resources. The definition is not specific to any one group nor does it exclude others. This definition is in accord with what Tore Bjorgo (2005a: 2) notes in that terrorism "is primarily an extremism of means, not one of ends." Definitions used by governments for legal purposes need to be more detailed and specific. Governments may want less precise definitions when dealing with foreign countries in order to avoid making unpopular decisions or extraditing individuals for terrorism to foreign governments. Terrorism is ultimately a form of psychological warfare that is designed to use fear to influence people. While guerrilla activity shares some similarity to terrorist attacks, guerrilla groups are more likely to attack military or police targets and only use terrorist tactics to supplement their other attacks.

KEY TERMS

anarchists, CIA, **extradition**, KGB, leaderless resistance, London transport bombings, Madrid train bombings, 9/11 attacks, Al Qaeda, Secret Intelligence Service, Unabomber

SUGGESTED READING

Badey, T. J. (1998) "Defining International Terrorism: A Pragmatic Approach," *Terrorism and Political Violence*, 10, 1: 90–107.

This article provides a useful and workable definition of terrorism on the international level.

Hoffman, B. (2006) *Inside Terrorism*, revised and expanded edition, New York: Columbia University Press.

This is an informative book providing coverage of terrorism in its various forms and a useful textbook that covers most aspects of terrorism.

Tan, A. H. T. (2006) *The Politics of Terrorism: A Survey*, London: Routledge.

This volume contains chapters dealing with various kinds of terrorism as well as an encyclopedic listing of terrorist movements and incidents.

Wilkinson, P. (1975) *Political Terrorism*, New York: Halstead Press.

This volume is an early, but comprehensive, book on terrorism that is still relevant.

2

WHAT DO TERRORISTS WANT?

Groups that resort to terrorism want to accomplish a wide variety of goals. These goals are often specific to a country, the target audience, the time period – in a word the political environment in which the groups operate. This chapter will first consider some suggestions about the root causes of terrorism that lead groups that seek change to rely on violence. There are a number of ways in which terrorist groups can be classified. First, they can be put into categories on the basis of what part of the political system they are trying to change – policies, political leadership, the structure of the political system, or the boundaries of the state. Second, they can be classified on the basis of their cause – religious issues, ethnic concerns, or ideological beliefs. It is also possible for governments to engage in terrorism against their citizens as noted in Chapter 1. Although the objectives for this kind of terrorism will be somewhat different, it is often undertaken or tolerated as part of an effort to achieve similar types of goals. Finally, it is worthwhile to discuss some of the distinctions between domestic terrorism and international terrorism.

CAUSES OF TERRORISM

Any discussion of the goals and objectives of terrorist groups needs to include some consideration of the possible underlying causes of terrorism. The question of causes, however, is a very complex one. Ultimately, there is no single cause or even a very small group of causes that would explain the level of terrorist activity. This lack of a single cause is in part due to the fact that terrorism is a technique that is available to all kinds of political groups that are disgruntled with the way things are in the current political environment. Groups unhappy with the current political circumstances will use other techniques (elections, military takeovers, bribery, etc.) if they are able to do so, but they will resort to terrorism if they lack these or other alternatives. Although there is no single cause of terrorism, there are a number of factors that appear to contribute to this type of violence in at least some cases.

Poverty has often been considered a basic cause of terrorism. It has been assumed that individuals are driven to engage in political violence because of their economic circumstances or because of the economic circumstances of the group they belong to. The poverty theory is an appealing one, and many terrorist groups cite social and economic injustices as justifications for their violence. While some studies have found a connection between poverty and terrorism, most have failed to find any direct connection (Maleckova 2005). It is not the poorest individuals who routinely join terrorist groups although some organizations may attract the poorer elements in society. Other groups tend to attract a more middle-class following, and other terrorist groups frequently draw upon cross-sections of the population in terms of economic well-being. Terrorist activity has not occurred in the poorest countries of the world or the ones with the greatest differences between rich and poor. While poverty may have a connection with terrorism, it is indirect and complex.

Another factor that has contributed to outbreaks of terrorism involves the strains associated with modernization and **globalization**. Globalization, like terrorism has been defined in many different ways. Most definitions agree on the key characteristic that it involves increasing connections among societies and cultures in terms of economic, social, political, and communications linkages. Ongoing changes in the world increasingly create problems for all societies, both rich and poor. Economic changes bring greater wealth and status to some groups, while other groups lose. Societies face the appearance of outside religions that threaten the existing domestic practices or the appearance of secular ideas that threaten the more religious elements in all countries. New ideas can also upset cultural or societal norms and patterns. Globalization also brings increased migration, and societies often react negatively to the presence of outsiders. The immigration debates in the United States and Europe in the first decade of the twenty-first century are just a recent example of the negative reactions to immigrants that can occur. With all these changes those who have lost as a consequence of the new circumstances may be tempted to resort to violence, including terrorism, to try to turn back the clock and to try to keep these changes from continuing.

A lack of opportunity for political participation has frequently been considered a cause of terrorism. Citizens become violent when other opportunities for political involvement are not available. While a lack of political participation has generated violence, including terrorism, truly repressive states with very limited participation (or none) have usually been able to prevent violence or have been able to quickly control it when it does occur. On the other hand democratic states with many opportunities for participation are often targets for terrorism. The civil liberties associated with democracies often provide advantages for terrorist groups. There are limits on the security forces and the techniques that can be used for dealing with suspected terrorists that are usually present. The use of the **Guantanamo Bay** base in Cuba by the United States to detain suspected terrorists is an obvious exception to such treatment. One of the reasons that the detention of suspects at the Guantanamo Bay facility has raised so much controversy is because it has been so contrary to democratic expectations. Freedom of movement facilitates attacks; freedom of press guarantees knowledge of their actions and influences the target audience, and the right to a fair trial means they may escape punishment even if they are caught. In democratic states the suspects in trials would even have the opportunity during the course of criminal proceedings to further publicize their cause. Of course, critics of democratic states, including those in some terrorist organizations, argue that democratic states do not provide real participation and equality or argue that the system is rigged against certain groups in society. It is also true that sometimes the rights that accused individuals are supposed to have are not honored as much as they should be. Even so, democracies do provide greater opportunities for terrorists precisely because they are more open.

Authoritarian states usually have been able to maintain control of actual and potential dissidents. The authorities and security forces do not have to worry about civil liberties or protecting the rights of persons suspected of terrorism. Surveillance methods and interrogation techniques can be virtually unrestricted in such systems. Even though such strategies of control can be harmful in the long term, not only to individual citizens but to state stability, they can prevent terrorism from occurring, or anyone engaging in terrorism can be quickly captured. Authoritarian states often are able to control to at least some extent how the media cover terrorist actions. In some cases they can even prevent any information about the terrorism from being publicized. During the existence of the Soviet Union, there were very few dissidents and virtually no terrorist episodes. The successor states to the Soviet Union, however, have faced many more difficulties and violent incidents. The most obvious example has been the problems that the Russian government has had with dissidents in Chechnya in the southern part of the country. The discontent in the region did not begin with the breakup of the Soviet Union; it was already present. The weaker Russian state that came into being, however has presented opportunities for Chechen dissidents that had not previously existed.

Another factor that has been suggested as contributing to outbreaks of terrorism has been the presence of relatively weak states that cannot effectively control their own territory. The lack of effective security forces whether in a democracy or a more authoritarian state provides opportunities for groups to organize and to launch attacks. Domestic groups can target weak states, or they can provide a safe base for groups from other countries that want to attack their home government. Lebanon in the 1970s and the 1980s and Somalia in the 1990s and the 2000s have sheltered a variety of terrorist organizations that used the lack of central authority to their own advantage. A factor that is related to weak states is the aftermath of wars (especially for the defeated countries) and economic deterioration. The breakup of empires or states can leave new countries weaker as well. It is no

Democratic systems and weak governments can contribute to the rise of terrorism. "Inefficiency or leniency can be found in a broad range of all but the most brutally efficient dictatorships, including incompetent authoritarian states . . . as well as modern liberal democratic states whose desire to protect civil liberties constrains security measures." (Crenshaw 2003: 94) surprise that many countries experienced political violence of all types in the aftermath of World War I and the Great Depression. Similarly, after World War II the weakened European colonial powers faced national liberation movements that they could no longer contain. The native populations in Cyprus, Aden, and Algeria, and the Jewish settler population in Palestine, for example, relied on terrorist attacks, usually in combination with other activities, to win their independence.

CHANGES IN POLICIES

Some terrorist groups seek changes in the domestic policies of a government. The groups may want fairer treatment for a particular group in society or they may want the government to follow domestic policies more in line with either conservative, more left-wing, or other political views. Anti-abortion groups in the United States are an example of such a group that has used violence to dispute the effects of a domestic policy. These groups are attempting to reverse the current policy of the United States government that permits abortions in some circumstances. Terrorist groups have also attacked targets linked to foreign governments in attempts to bring about changes in foreign policies. Al Qaeda and groups influenced by it have as one of their objectives changes in the foreign policies of the United States and its allies. These groups want changes in policies towards the Middle East and Muslim states, including at least partial Western withdrawal from Muslim areas. Anti-Castro Cuban exile groups are another example. These groups attacked targets associated with foreign governments that had recognized or could be seen as supporting Cuba. Many other exile groups have launched attacks seeking to undermine foreign support for their home governments.

CHANGES IN POLITICAL LEADERSHIP

Sometimes groups seek not only changes in the policies of the government in power, but also changes in the associated group that is in power in the government. The objective of the group goes beyond the removal of just one leader. An assassination could remove a single individual to be replaced by another, but with terrorism, groups are seeking a change in the political elite. They may be seeking to drive out a particular portion of the political elite to be replaced by another or to create conditions that are more likely to bring a new group (ethnic, religious, political beliefs) into power. There have been groups in the past that hoped to place different groups into power by using a campaign of terrorism. Some of the opposition groups in Iraq have sought to bring about changes in the groups that are in power in the new government of that country. Of course, there is usually an expectation in all of these cases that there will be changes in policy that come with changes in leadership. Groups may hope to bring about changes in the leadership of foreign governments as well if they see such an alteration as being likely to bring about the changes in policies that they prefer.

CHANGES IN THE POLITICAL SYSTEM

When groups are willing or feel compelled to resort to violence, they are frequently seeking more than policy changes or a different set of political leaders. They are more likely to want to bring about major changes in the political system itself. They may hope to replace a military regime or a one-party government with a democratic system. In other cases the groups may want to replace a monarchy with a republic or reestablish a monarchy to replace a republic. The Islamic Republic in Iran when it was first established had to deal with terrorist attacks from groups that wanted to establish a more secular system in that country. Groups from the left have sought to overthrow the existing government and to replace it with a government based on the principles expounded by Marx and Lenin. Groups from the right, on the other hand, have sought to overturn governments of the left. The ultimate objective of the anti-Castro exile groups that operated outside Cuba was a complete change in the nature of the Cuban government.

CHANGES IN STATE BOUNDARIES

The final change in underlying political circumstances that terrorist groups may be seeking involves geographic goals. Anti-colonial movements seek to create independent states that are no longer parts of the empires that contained them. In other cases regional groups will use terrorism in an attempt to break away from existing states and create new nations. In yet other situations a group may seek to have a portion of a country attached to a different state, as was the case when the **Irish Republican Army** (IRA) wanted to unite Northern Ireland with the Irish Republic after the two parts of the island were separated after World War I. The changes in boundaries may imply a change in the political system as well as a change in boundaries, although it is possible that those seeking the changes may not have issues with the form of government. They may be willing to establish the same form for the new state. Boundary changes would, of course, require a change in the political leadership and undoubtedly some policy changes as well.

RELIGIOUS GOALS

Many of the terrorist groups that have appeared had objectives that have been based in their religious views. Al Qaeda has sought policy changes within Islamic countries and changes in their political systems and changes in the foreign policies of other countries. In some cases the religious group may have sought or may be seeking to reduce secular influences and to introduce more religious laws into the land. Extreme Islamic groups in a number of countries have sought to force the incorporation of more Islamic prescriptions into national legal codes. Other religious groups have sought to gain autonomy for their religion or greater rights for their group within a country where they might have been facing discrimination due to their minority position. Protestants in New Guinea and Indonesia, Muslims in southern Thailand, Sikhs in India, and Christians and followers of traditional religions in the southern Sudan have all, at times, relied on violent attacks and terrorism in what they perceived as efforts to protect their religious groups. Anti-abortion groups in the United States have also been motivated by religious beliefs.

It is also possible for members of the dominant religious group to use violence against minority religious groups, often in efforts to drive them out of the country or out of a given area. Extreme Hindu groups in India have launched attacks against members of other religions as part of their efforts to incorporate more elements of Hinduism into national laws and culture and to drive out what they see as intrusive and contaminating foreign influences. Muslims in Indonesia have attacked the Christian minorities in some areas of the country since they are seen as obstacles to creating a more Islamic state. The Mormons in the United States before the Civil War were driven out of New York, Ohio, Missouri, and Illinois in succession by the dominant Christian communities because they were different and considered even potentially subversive.

ETHNIC OR NATIONALIST GOALS

Terrorist groups also can be motivated by ethnic or nationalist concerns. Minority ethnic groups may become dissatisfied with their position in particular states, and some members may turn to terrorism as part of an effort to gain autonomy or independence. Groups could also have more limited goals. They might want policy changes such as the ending of discrimination or they might desire guarantees of greater representation in the ruling circles. Any of these desired changes could require some changes in the political system to accommodate such guarantees or inclusion of previously excluded groups.

The majority group may also engage in terrorism targeting ethnic minorities because they are feared or disliked. The majority may wish to repress the minority, or they could attempt to prevent the minority from creating an independent state or having a particular region joined to a neighboring country. The actions by the majority group may eventually reach the level of **ethnic cleansing** where there is an effort to drive out those that are "different". Such efforts will invariably rely on spreading terrorism among the members of the targeted group. **Genocide** is the ultimate form of ethnic cleansing, but it is not terrorism since it seeks to eliminate the target population rather than spread terror among the members. Most other forms of ethnic cleansing, however, simply seek the removal of the targeted group. Fear is an important part of the motivation to drive them away, and the members of the groups are, in fact, permitted to leave.

IDEOLOGICAL GOALS

Ideologies are frequently referred to as left and right or left-wing and right-wing. Although there are many variations, **left-wing ideologies** seek to promote greater equality for individuals in society. They are opposed to hierarchy and opposed to great differences in economic wealth. Ideologies of the left include communism and its variations, socialism, anarchism, and labor (and in the United States liberalism). **Right-wing ideologies** accept greater inequalities as natural and expected in society, support existing institutions, often have connections to more religious elements in society, and favor the status quo. Right-wing ideologies include conservatism, Christian democracy, and monarchism. Most left-wing and right-wing ideologies, of course, do not promote a reliance on violence, but the more extreme versions of both groups often do support the use of violence as a means of obtaining objectives. Any of these ideologies and others could serve as a basis for violent activities under the right circumstances, such as might occur when battling against an authoritarian, repressive government that espoused different political views.

Terrorist groups whose reason for existence is rooted in ideology seldom seek to change state boundaries whether they are of the right or the left. What they often seek to change is the nature of the political system. Even when they do not want to change the system, they want changes in the political leadership so that it would be more inclusive of elements of the society that they see as unfairly excluded. They also inevitably want to bring about policy changes. Extreme left-wing groups in the past, such as the anarchists, attacked the class structure and the privileges of the existing system. Violent leftists that appeared in Latin America, Western Europe, and elsewhere in the 1960s and later were opposed to the inequities of domestic and international capitalism. More recently environmental and animal rights groups have appeared to fight the ecological damage done by capitalism. Extreme right-wing groups have fought against changes in society. The various fascist parties (including the Nazis in Germany as an extreme case) sought to prevent socialism and other new political views from gaining strength. Violent groups on the right more recently have targeted migrants because of the groups' opposition to foreign religions, foreign cultures, different races, and different ideas.

COMBINATIONS OF OBJECTIVES

While many of the groups that resort to terrorism can be seen as primarily ethnic, religious, or ideological, some groups are more difficult to place in just one category, and, of course, it is not necessary to do so. These groups have mixed motives and objectives. In many areas of the world, for example, terrorist groups have formed alliances of convenience with criminal organizations, especially those involved in drug trafficking. Both the criminal groups and the political dissidents opposed to the government in power benefit when the government is weak. The long-term goals of the criminals and political opponents may not be in agreement, but cooperation is in their mutual interests in the short term. The alliance between the drug cartels and leftist groups in Colombia has been one of the most obvious cases of such cooperation. The government of Colombia has yet to come up with an effective way of combating this alliance, and the drug producers and leftists continue to control significant portions of the country.

In other cases, religion and ethnicity overlap and reinforce each other. While the rebels in Chechnya in Russia are often portrayed as Islamic radicals, their battle really began as a national struggle for independence. The Chechens are overwhelmingly Islamic in culture (and often in practice as well), and they eventually began to receive assistance from external Islamic organizations. This support in turn has led to greater emphasis on Islamic themes among the rebel groups that are fighting the Russians. In Northern Ireland, the violence was often seen to be a consequence of religious differences between Protestants and Catholics. In reality the conflict is also between those inhabitants who see themselves as British (overwhelmingly affiliated with Protestantism even if loosely) and those who consider themselves Irish (overwhelmingly Catholic). The struggle at times has even involved elements of ideology since the dissident groups have emphasized the differences between the economic status of the Catholic Irish (much more likely to be working class and with a lower standard of living) and the

Protestant British (much more likely to be middle class and with a higher average standard of living).

Another factor that makes it difficult to classify some terrorist groups in terms of underlying objectives is due to the fact that the multiple characteristics reflect changes over time. A group may attach ideological components to their ethnic or religious goals or see ethnic or religious implications of their ideologies. Anti-colonial groups in the old European empires could see their struggle as both nationalist and as part of an effort to resist domination and exploitation by capitalist groups in the colonizing power. The basis of support in the population may also change over time, requiring a re-orientation of the propaganda of the dissident group. Most terrorist leaders are, after all, politicians, even if of an unusual type, and they may shift their appeals and goals to keep popular support or generate additional support.

GOVERNMENT TERRORISM

As was mentioned in Chapter 1 and as will be discussed in some detail in Chapter 6, governments will support or permit the use of terrorism against their own citizens. Governments have some of the same types of objectives as dissident groups. They are unlikely, however, to be supporters of terrorism to bring about changes in political leadership, policy changes, or changes in the political system. Just the opposite is true – the government is using the violence as part of attempts to preserve policies, the system, and especially the leadership. The terrorism is likely to be directed against opposition groups that are seeking changes in these areas. If a government is too weak to use repression against the political opposition it may rely on terror.

When governments attack domestic opponents it will frequently be on ideological grounds since the disagreements on policy changes and the political system will often have an ideological component. Governments may seek to expand the borders of a state, but they are unlikely to attack their own citizens to achieve any changes in national boundaries. They may, however, seek to deal with domestic groups that they fear to avoid threats to the integrity of the state. The suspect groups inside the borders could be ethnic or religious minorities. If the government cannot rely on open repression or expulsion, it may employ less direct means to dominate the group. In other cases, the government could reflect a majority view towards ethnic or religious minorities where they are disliked because of their differences and become targets for that reason. A weak government may find it convenient to overlook such attacks since they might deflect attention from the governmental shortcomings or because the unpopular minority provides a convenient target. The monarchy in Russia prior to World War I, for example, acquiesced in attacks against its own Jewish citizens since they absorbed some of the blame for the failures of the government.

DOMESTIC VERSUS INTERNATIONAL TERRORISM

Frequently, a distinction has been made in the past between foreign and domestic terrorism. Domestic terrorists attack targets in their own country and avoid foreign property and personnel. International terrorists (1) attack foreign targets in their own country, (2) attack foreign targets abroad, or (3) attack targets associated with their home governments such as an embassy or a government company in a foreign country. The last possibility is clearly international since it crosses state boundaries, but it is really an extension of the dissident group's problems with their own government.

To the extent that the distinction between domestic and international terrorism is valid, domestic terrorists seek to bring about changes in the policies of their government, in the political leadership, or in the political system. If they are a regional or ethnic group seeking to create a new state or join themselves to a neighboring state, then they may also be seeking to change state boundaries. International terrorists can have the same aims in some cases as when they target symbols of the government abroad. They may also target a foreign country if the government of that country is aiding their own government. They are hoping to change the foreign policy of the external government to give themselves a better chance of bringing about the domestic changes they desire. The more international terrorist groups may attack a foreign government in efforts to bring about other policy changes. Al Qaeda wants to lessen US involvement in the Middle East and other Islamic areas. The Madrid train attacks in 2004 and the attacks in the London transport bombings in 2005 by militants identifying with al Qaeda were intended to convince the Spanish and British governments to withdraw their support for the United States in the Middle East. It also seeks to stop Western support of the repressive governments in power in Middle Eastern countries. These repressive governments are also seen as being too secular and not following religious law closely enough. Some of the leftist groups that operated in the latter part of the twentieth century regarded international capitalism and capitalist states as their enemies and sought to undermine the effects that capitalism was having.

It is indeed becoming more difficult to distinguish between domestic and international terrorism. Domestic terrorism increasingly has international implications in a more interconnected world. International terrorism has implications for a government in the country where the attack takes place, in the country where the terrorists originated, and sometimes for other countries as well. While it has become more difficult to separate domestic from international terrorism in any precise way, it is important to note that the vast majority of terrorist actions that do occur are primarily domestic in terms of the objectives they are seeking. It is the international terrorist acts, however, that attract more attention since they involve more than one country. These attacks, therefore, often generate greater publicity, which may be an important aim for the terrorist group itself. Attacks in democratic countries with freedom of press coverage can be especially important in this regard. While the international incidents are still only a small portion of the attacks that occur, it is the international incidents that are likely to be more deadly on average than the domestic attacks (Enders and Sandler 2000: 327–8).

CONCLUSIONS

Terrorist groups pursue a wide variety of objectives. They may seek to have domestic governments or foreign governments (or both) change policies; they seek changes in domestic leadership or government systems; they attempt to change state boundaries. Many groups have goals that are linked to ethnic ideals for autonomy or independence, while others have goals imbedded in religious beliefs or ideological convictions. Some groups reflect combinations of these motivations. Further, governments may resort to terrorist actions against their own citizens with the same types of motivations as dissident groups. Ultimately, many different groups with many different goals have operated and continue to operate using terrorism as a technique in efforts to achieve these different objectives because terrorism as a technique is available to all the groups.

KEY TERMS

ethnic cleansing, genocide, globalization, **government terrorism**, left-wing ideology, right-wing ideology

FURTHER READING

Bjorgo, T. (ed.) (2005) *Root Causes of Terrorism: Myths, Reality, and Ways Forward*, London: Routledge.

This volume provides a valuable overview of possible causes of terrorism and also contains chapters dealing with the types of goals terrorist groups pursue.

Laqueur, W. (2001) *A History of Terrorism*. New Brunswick, NJ: Transaction Publishers.

This book provides a succinct review of terrorism through the ages by one of the academics who has been involved in the study of the subject for over twenty years.

Lutz, J. M. and B. J. Lutz (2008) *Global Terrorism*, 2nd edn, London: Routledge.

This textbook relies on numerous cases studies to introduce various aspects of terrorism including classifications and causes.

Richardson, L. (ed.) (2006) *The Roots of Terrorism*, London: Routledge.

This edited volume discusses causes in terms of background issues such as economics, democracy, religion, and globalization.

3

WHO BECOMES A TERRORIST?

A great deal of effort has been made to determine who is likely to become a terrorist or who is likely to be successfully recruited by an existing group. These efforts are particularly important to security forces or anyone else involved in counterterrorism efforts since the ability to identify persons likely to join such groups would be quite valuable. There are, however, relatively few predictors available, although there are some patterns that can be discerned. As noted in Chapter 2, poverty is not a very good predictor of who will join a group, but there are some characteristics related to age, gender, psychological characteristics, and motivations that have been considered as relevant. These characteristics also vary somewhat for religious, ethnic, and ideological groups.

PSYCHOLOGICAL PROFILE

It has often been assumed that many terrorists have psychological problems – that they are even crazy. These psychological problems are then assumed to lead them to participate in attacks in which innocent individuals are killed more or less indiscriminately. We do not have anything approaching a detailed or complete sample of terrorists since they keep their identities hidden as much as possible. There has been enough information gathered on those involved in many groups to know that very few of the individuals have any significant psychological problems. There is no evidence

Frederick J. Hacker (1976), an American psychologist, once classified terrorists as crusaders, criminals, or crazies, a view that much of the public would probably accept as accurate.

that persons suffering from mental disorders are overrepresented in the ranks of terrorists, even though there may be individuals with problems in some groups. It is possible that some groups are willing to use individuals with psychological problems at times, but they cannot rely on them because their mental disorders make them potentially unstable and poor security risks for the organization. As a consequence, in psychological terms individuals who join terrorist groups are disturbingly normal.

Not even suicide terrorists display backgrounds that would suggest any prevalence of psychological problems. Suicide attackers and would-be suicide attackers have not displayed suicidal tendencies as individuals. They appear to volunteer for suicide missions in order to advance the cause of the group. There is no evidence that they have deep-seated death wishes or any other psychological characteristics that pre-dispose them as a group towards participating in these attacks. Involvement in suicide attacks has also not been confined to individuals who are particularly religious. The **Tamil Tigers**, a dissident ethnic group in Sri Lanka, was for a long time the group that most frequently used suicide attacks. Many of the suicide attacks in Lebanon as well as Israel and the Occupied Territories have been by members of secular political groups, not by members of religious organizations. It is true that more recently suicide attacks have become the trademark of Islamic extremists, but it is important to note that the dominant use of this technique by religious groups is actually a rather new phenomenon.

It has also been suggested that terrorists can be criminals. Just as persons with psychological problems are unlikely to be part of terrorist groups, criminals – or more appropriately opportunists – are also unlikely to join a violent organization with political objectives. By definition, criminals usually seek financial gain, and terrorist groups provide few opportunities in this area since most terrorist groups are weak and are likely to fail. The groups that have a chance of success, however slim, can attract some opportunistic adherents when a group is on the upswing. When criminal organizations have cooperated with terrorist groups, the ultimate goal of the criminal groups has been to improve their opportunities for financial gain by weakening the government or police. It is possible for some individuals with limited prospects in their society to join because there is an opportunity for food, shelter, and support that might not otherwise exist.

Opportunism can take many forms beyond direct involvement in a group. Merchants or professionals might find it expedient to support a group in order to continue to conduct their business or practice their trade since the lack of support could lead to losses in the business sector. Participation in a group might also provide status in other ways that could be useful in a conventional political career or in business. In the southern states in the United States, many people joined the **Ku Klux Klan** (KKK), a group that frequently practiced terrorism, since it provided useful personal contacts in business and other areas. In other situations where members of terrorist groups are seen as heroes or defenders of a particular portion of the population, individuals might gain status from membership. While individuals who join or support a group for these reasons might be important for the organization, they are unlikely to be a large element in most cases. Opportunists, like criminals, will weigh the costs and benefits of participating, and quite often they are likely to conclude that the costs will outweigh any potential benefits.

A particular group of individuals who qualify as criminals that has been attracted to dissident causes have been individuals from prison populations. When activists from ideological struggles have been caught and imprisoned for their activities, they have often been able to attract followers in prison. Leftists have been able to argue convincingly that the criminal justice system unfairly targets the poor or discriminates against workers and peasants. Right-wing groups, such as the **Aryan Nations** in the United States, have also had some successes with white prison populations by arguing that the political and social systems have been changed to devalue the worth and contributions of those holding true conservative (or even reactionary) views and values and that they have devalued the white race. Extreme religious groups have frequently been able to recruit new members as well. Religions and ideologies provide guiding principles and social structures that support the individuals while they are in prison. A significant number of prisoners in Europe have converted to Islam and have become involved in more radical and violent groups in some cases. The ones who are recruited in these

"Prisons form a primary ground for both radicalization and recruitment … In terms of radicalization, prisons are in themselves environments conducive to the radicalization of alienated individuals who have dismissed society and are in search of a new or higher purpose in life." (Korteweg *et al.* 2010: 32)

situations are not normally the professional criminals; they are much more likely to be petty criminals who have had economic problems or difficulties in terms of fitting in with their societies. These recruits, however, do not join the terrorist groups for financial gain, so they are not the criminal element that Hacker referred to in this threefold typology of terrorists as noted in the Box at the beginning of this chapter, nor are these individuals obviously opportunists.

Terrorist groups can at times provide a sense of belonging for members and give individuals support that they might otherwise not have. The provision of a support structure is a necessary component for most groups, but there is no evidence that terrorist groups in general disproportionately attract rootless individuals seeking a group identity. Analyses have found that over time, members of many groups do become very dependent on the group for a social network and emotional support since they often become increasingly isolated from the broader society. Solidarity with the group becomes increasingly important for the members, and as a consequence, it is often difficult for long-standing members to exit the group and re-integrate into society. Isolation within the group may create psychological problems for members, but these problems appear after individuals have joined, not as a cause for joining.

Crusader was the last category noted by Hacker. This term refers to those who are committed to the cause that the organization is pursuing. Most members of virtually all terrorist groups would be believers in the cause. Opportunists are unlikely to join a group with small chances of success. Believers in the cause in contrast would display above average dedication to the political objectives of the violent group. The willingness to use violence would also seem to require a higher level of commitment or belief. Thus, the one characteristic of individuals who join terrorist groups is their level of commitment, and this characteristic clearly dominates when compared to those who are opportunists – including criminals – and those with psychological problems. Unfortunately, in the efforts to profile likely members of groups, there are neither key predictors of commitment nor predictors as to which individuals with the appropriate level of dedication are likely to join a group and which individuals are not likely to do so.

OTHER CHARACTERISTICS

While persons involved in terrorist groups do not fit a psychological profile, there are some other tendencies that have been observed. One societal situation that has been linked to circumstances that can attract individuals to extreme causes involves the condition known as **anomie**. A person in this situation, and "an anomic individual", is someone who has been displaced from a comfortable or supporting social structure into new circumstances that are unstructured for them and may even be chaotic. Persons who move from rural villages with a clear social and economic structure to urban areas may find themselves without a solid base. Immigrants moving to a new country can face even greater adjustment problems. Prison populations would also include many individuals who would be considered anomic, even though prison itself will usually provide some structure. The disruption that comes with major wars can also create the potential for an increase in the number of anomic individuals. Persons who find themselves in this situation can be veterans, people displaced by the fighting, or other civilians who find their social and economic structures disrupted. The dislocations that come with the economic, social, and cultural changes associated with globalization and modernization can also create anomie. All of the individuals in anomic situations can be attracted to a variety of organizations, including radical and violent ones. The individuals provide a potential pool of recruits for dissident terrorist groups or even for organizations using violence on behalf of governments or groups in power. Even though anomic individuals may be more susceptible to the appeals of radical groups, most of them do not join.

The terrorist groups can provide a sense of belonging for its members, including those from anomic situations, and give individuals support groups that they might otherwise lack. The provision of a support structure is a necessary component for most groups, but there is no evidence that terrorist groups in general disproportionately attract rootless individuals seeking a group identity. Analyses have found that over time, members of many groups do become very dependent on the group for a social network and emotional support since they often become increasingly isolated from the broader society. Solidarity within the group becomes increasingly important for the members, and as a consequence, it is often difficult for long-standing members to exit from the group and re-integrate into society. Isolation within the group may create psychological problems for members, but these problems appear after the individuals have joined, they are not a cause for joining.

It would appear that to some extent terrorist groups involve teens and younger adults and older adults (as well as the very young, of course) are underrepresented. This tendency is hardly surprising since the demands of active involvement are more easily met by younger individuals. The active terrorists are similar to the rank and file of the regular military in regard to their age. The leadership cadres of terrorist groups, however, often involve older, and perhaps less physically fit, individuals. The older age of the leader is not surprising, especially for groups that have survived for a number of years. The age difference for the leadership that is often present corresponds in some ways to the higher ranks of the regular military or police where experience is valued. Older individuals are also less likely to be active in terrorist groups, at least in terms of carrying out attacks for other reasons, since they are more likely to have family or other responsibilities that limit opportunities for involvement. While activists involved in groups may be younger on average, an organization rooted in a particular portion of the population may be supported by people of all ages in terms of safe house, food, clothing, money and information. In such cases, the age of the activists would simply reflect a pragmatic concern over strength and other physical factors rather than any special appeal that the organization would have for the young.

As was discussed in the previous chapter, members of terrorist groups are not particularly poor or deprived. Similarly, they are not noteworthy for low levels of education. They do not fit the stereotype as poor and uneducated individuals. Many groups attract individuals who are representative of a more general population in terms of education, or in some cases persons who are even better educated on average than the general population. While there are some variations among types of terrorist organizations and even among groups in the same category, neither a lack of education nor advanced education consistently explains why people choose to join a terrorist group.

Active members of terrorist groups are much more likely to be males, just as the regular military is a predominately male organization. Women typically have not often been in the "front lines," for social, cultural, or religious reasons, but they have often been valuable in support roles and in gathering intelligence. Women, however, have become more important in many organizations, and they have increasingly become involved in attacks themselves. Women have some advantages when they undertake operations. They often have easier access to target areas because security forces may consider them to be less suspicious. It will often be awkward, for example, for security personnel to search women at checkpoints. Groups have also been willing to use women in suicide attacks for similar practical reasons. While the active ranks of terrorist groups are still largely male, female activists have begun to be more involved in a much wider range of activities.

NATIONALIST/ETHNIC GROUPS

Terrorist groups based in an ethnic or national movement or seeking ethnic or nationalist goals, of course, tend to attract members from that ethnic group or nationality. Even though there may be sympathetic and dedicated outsiders or opportunists from other segments of the population, the goals of the organization will pretty well define the available membership. If an organization is seeking autonomy or independence, they may have at least the tacit support of a portion or almost all the ethnic population. The population or large portions of it may disagree with the terrorist tactics of the group, but they may still identify with the overall objectives. This situation may make it more difficult for security or police forces to gather intelligence from informants or to isolate the violent group from the rest of the population, at least in cases where the ethnic population has real or perceived grievances with the government in power.

While ethnic terrorist groups reflect the tendency towards younger and male activists, they often incorporate broader elements of the population, and support for the organizations may often be a reflection of this base population in terms of age and education. Groups like the Tamil Tigers and the Palestinian Liberation Organization (PLO) have been willing to use women in at least some of their operations. During the terror campaign against the French authorities and the European settlers in colonial Algeria in the late 1950s, the Algerian National Liberation Front cells frequently used women who could pass for French to penetrate into European areas and plant bombs. The Tamil Tigers have used women in suicide attacks with some regularity. Violent Chechen groups, which were initially clearly nationalist but which also later incorporated religious elements, have also been representative of the broader population. These Chechen groups also relied on women, even as suicide bombers. These **black widows** suicide bombers were women who had lost husbands or sometimes other family members to Russian forces. Their attacks represented an effort to gain vengeance against the enemy. Women suicide bombers have been used against Russian troops in Chechnya itself, and there were at least two suicide attacks in which women destroyed Russian airliners.

The fact that Chechen groups have been willing to use women as suicide attackers is one indication that many of the dissident organizations in the region are more nationalist than religious. Islamic groups have been very reluctant to use women in this fashion, and some Islamic groups continue to refuse to let women serve as martyrs in suicide attacks.

RELIGIOUS GROUPS

Religious organizations sometimes are seen as being composed of especially committed individuals who are driven by their spiritual values. Obviously, some of the members of religious groups are extremely dedicated, but it has yet to be proven that religious groups consistently have more committed members than other types of organizations. It has also not just been religious groups that have been able to find volunteers for suicide attacks as noted. What does seem to be true for terrorist groups based in religion is that they are often willing to inflict casualties on outsiders, since those who believe differently (including those with secular beliefs) have placed themselves in opposition to God by their failure to adhere to the appropriate beliefs. The actions of the outsiders (or their inaction if they are not following prescribed patterns) place them within the target population. In many cases, however, the targets are not members of other religions but members of the same religious community who either follow somewhat different practices or who do not follow the more extreme or fundamentalist version of the same religion. Conflicts among Sunni and Shia in the Muslim world or between Protestants and Catholics in the Christian community are obvious examples of this phenomenon.

Members of terrorist groups rooted in religion often are representative of broader populations in terms of membership as are ethnic groups, but there are some important differences. While activists tend to be young, at least some religious groups involve older activists as well. Religious groups have also often attracted educated individuals. It was assumed that exposure to more education would weaken religious ties, but that has not always happened. It is possible that some of the more educated members have joined religious groups when they have difficulty finding employment commensurate with their education in job markets in those instances where the supply of graduates exceeds the available positions. There are a number of Islamic groups that have been quite successful in attracting college graduates. Sikhs in India involved in a terrorist and guerrilla campaign against the government have included individuals with all levels of education. Similarly, the Muslim groups that fought a terrorist and guerrilla war against the government of Algeria in the 1990s involved a number of persons with university educations. More recently, young men who see themselves as part of al Qaeda and participants in the global jihad have included individuals who are in economically marginal jobs and who are less well educated than similar activists have been in the past. These activists are also frequently members of small, close-knit groups whose attitudes reinforce each other (Atran 2008). Some of these recent activists are different from some of the other groups linked with Al Qaeda. The diversity of supporters, however, has indicated that Islamic religious activists have come from many different sectors of society.

Many religious groups have been less likely to involve women as activists. In part, this reluctance is due to the fact that a number of religions in their more fundamentalist versions have been interpreted to place women in secondary roles. Religious groups that are reacting to changes that occur with globalization and modernization are more likely to adhere to such views. Islamic groups have been male dominated as well, but at least some of these groups have shown an increasing willingness to involve women in the actual terrorist actions. The disparate collection of American Christian religious groups that have used occasional terrorist violence have almost always been male dominated or exclusively male. On the whole, religious organizations would appear to be much less likely on average to involve women in actual attacks than some other types of groups.

There are two distinct types of religious individuals who may be more likely to join a terrorist group. The first group consists of recent converts who often are the most adamant in their belief patterns. A second group with a similar potential has been the offspring of immigrants in societies where the majority religion is different. These individuals frequently find themselves isolated in their new communities. They do not or cannot integrate into the

The **Aum Shinrikyo** cult in Japan was able to attract educated individuals with advanced degrees to its ranks. Many of these individuals with scientific training were involved in the efforts to develop weapons of mass destruction.

majority society, and they turn to religious communities instead for a social or support network. These two groups in Western Europe have been seen as a source of members for violent Islamic groups. The London transport attacks were launched by second generation Muslims who identified with global jihad. Richard Reid, the man who tried to use a shoe bomb on a flight from France to the United States and many of the individuals in the United States who have been arrested for involvement in terrorist conspiracies have been converts.

IDEOLOGICAL GROUPS

Left-wing and right-wing ideological groups tend to be different in many ways in terms of the characteristics of the activists. They are similar to each other and to other terrorist organizations in that they attract younger individuals. The leadership may be older, but some of the extreme left-wing groups such as the **Red Army Faction** in Germany the Red Brigades in Italy, and groups in Argentina had relatively youthful leaders, in part because the groups attracted and were largely composed of students. Right-wing groups, on the other hand seem to usually have older leaders even if many of the activists are young.

The two types of groups have often differed in terms of the education of the members. Left-wing groups have frequently included large numbers of university students or recent graduates. Organizations in Europe, Latin America, and the Weathermen in the United States drew heavily upon such students. The middle class and secular groups that launched attacks against the Islamic Republic in Iran in its first two years of its existence also had a large number of students in their ranks. Environmental activists involved in property attacks against targets considered to be doing ecological damage seem to have attracted such individuals as well. It is clear that more mainstream environmental groups have had greater appeal to those with more education. Right-wing groups, on the other hand, appear to attract individuals with lower levels of education on average. Many of the activists in these groups face limited economic prospects, and they often blame their situation on competition from migrant communities. They can also be victims of modernization and thus susceptible to political views that tout a return to the ideas of a better past and join conservative groups as a response. Not all right-wing groups have the characteristic of appealing to the uneducated or undereducated. In the past, European fascist parties, which often relied on terror tactics, did include more educated individuals. In part these organization attracted middle-class individuals who feared the victory of communism or socialism and greater power for the working classes. Thus, the educational characteristics of the right-wing organizations have varied in different periods of time. This variation seems to have been dependent at least in part on which groups have felt threatened by impending changes occurring from broader currents or events.

There are also differences between the left and the right in terms of the involvement of women in the groups. Women have played a more prominent role in left-wing terrorist groups. They were part of the anarchist groups in Russia in the late 1800s and early 1900s, and they were even members of plots to kill the czar. Women were often involved in the student groups that were active in Western Europe, Latin America, and the United States. Ulrike Mienhof was the co-founder with Andreas Baader of the Red Army Faction (better known as the Baader-Meinhof Gang). Activists in environmental groups have also included women. It is more difficult to find examples of women playing similarly important roles in right-wing groups. The activists are almost always men although women have joined and supported their male counterparts. They have perhaps been most active in Scandinavian countries (where in general women have achieved greater equality with men than most areas of the world), although there is little evidence that they have been involved in direct attacks.

Members of left-wing and right-wing groups do differ from ethnic and religious groups in one important respect. Membership of an ethnic group is often predetermined, and individuals may not support a terrorist group, but they still remain linked to it by a common heritage. While individuals can, and do, change religious affiliations, in many contexts religious identification is relatively fixed as well. Only cults such as Aum Shinriyko have an element of conscious choice for the members. The decision to identify with an ideology, however, is more fluid and subject to choice. Similarly, there is more flexibility in deciding to join the terrorist fringe of either ideological camp that is chosen. This circumstance makes it more difficult for the terrorist group to develop a support base or recruit activists in a population because the natural linkage present with ethnicity and often with religion is absent. It may also explain why ideological terrorist organizations on average usually lack the longevity of religious or ethnic groups (Tan 2000: 268).

GOVERNMENT REPRESSION

There is one group of individuals who do appear to be much more likely to join violent dissident groups. This tendency is true for ethnic, religious, and ideological groups. Individuals who have lost family members or close friends to the military, police, or security forces often join violent opposition groups to avenge the death of individuals close to them (Silke 2005: 245). Similarly, individuals with no link to terrorist groups are likely to join such groups if they have been vigorously questioned by the police or security forces and mistreated or tortured in the process. They seek vengeance for what was inflicted upon them. As mentioned above, the Chechen black widow suicide bombers are examples of individuals who fit into this category. Members of Palestinian groups, whether secular or religious, often include persons who have suffered at the hands of the security forces or lost loved ones. Government efforts to uncover and deal with terrorist groups often unintentionally serve as an aid to recruitment. Even successful actions against known terrorists can lead to new recruits joining the organization. A vicious circle starts in which government repression leads to individuals joining terrorist groups which launch more attacks that generate more repression, etc. Government security forces and police face the dilemma of taking insufficient action, thereby permitting terrorist groups to continue to operate, or if they become too vigorous in their efforts to find terrorists, they risk turning suspects into recruits. Of course, heavy-handed repression has sometimes defeated terrorist groups, but often action within the rule of law involving fair trials and respect for the rights of defendants and suspects can often eliminate or at least reduce the dangers of government actions creating new terrorists.

CONCLUSIONS

Terrorist groups have attracted a wide variety of individuals. For the most part, they do not suffer from psychological problems nor are they opportunists or criminals. They are almost always individuals who are committed to the cause that the group espouses. The one category of individuals likely to join a violent group is those who have lost a loved one to government forces or suffered some other major personal loss or indignity. Beyond this group, those who join terrorist organizations are more likely to be male, and they are frequently young. Other than these rather basic attributes, there are few commonalities. There are some differences among various kinds of terrorist organizations, although not all the groups in the same category are similar. Members of leftist groups often include more educated individuals; members of ethnic or religious groups are often cross-sections of the broader populations; members of right-wing groups in many cases are less well-educated. Women generally appear to play a greater role in left-wing groups and at least some ethnic groups. Recent converts to a religion or second generation migrants in religiously different societies may be more susceptible to extremist appeals. Ultimately, these generalizations, while important, are not especially helpful since most members of any category (age, gender, education or not, occupation, recent convert, or even those who have suffered losses) will not become members of violent groups, even if they sympathize with them. Thus, it remains quite difficult to identify or to predict which individuals are terrorists or are likely to become terrorists.

KEY TERMS

Aum Shinrikyo, black widows, Red Army Faction, Red Brigades, Tamil Tigers

FURTHER READING

Horgan, J. (2003), "The Search for the Terrorist Personality," in A. Silke (ed.), *Terrorists, Victims, and Society: Psychological Perspectives on Terrorism and Its Consequences.* Chichester: Wiley, 3–27.

This chapter details some of the difficulties involved in trying to determine who is likely to become a terrorist.

Kuznar, L. A. and J. M. Lutz (2007), "Risk Sensitivity and Terrorism," *Political Studies*, 55, 2: 341–61.

This article provides an useful discussion of some of the factors that would lead groups to support terrorist groups.

Leiken, R. S. (2005), "Europe's Angry Muslims," *Foreign Affairs*, 84, 4: 120–35.

This article assesses the danger from recent converts and second generation Muslim immigrants in Europe, suggesting that these individuals are more likely to join terrorist organizations.

WHAT ARE THE TECHNIQUES?

Terrorism itself consists of a number of distinct strategies and a wide variety of tactical techniques. Which techniques are used by which groups have varied by time and circumstance. Terrorist organizations have proven that they are quite adaptable. They have adopted whatever tactics are available to them, which fit the situations they are facing. Five broad or general strategies that terrorist organizations have used and continue to use will be discussed below. That discussion will be followed by a consideration of the various tactics that may be used by groups as well as the kinds of weaponry that terrorist organizations have relied upon.

STRATEGIES OF TERRORISM

A number of different kinds of strategies have been attributed to terrorist groups. At times groups have made their basic strategies very public. At other times the strategies have to be inferred from their actions, even though there are some situations where the terrorist group may have intentionally misled the public or the government as to their methods or objectives. In these cases, information that is available later will clarify the basic strategy that was being pursued. Kydd and Walter (2006) have suggested that terrorist organizations over time have followed five basic strategies. The five strategies that they identify are (1) attrition, (2) intimidation, (3) provocation, (4) spoiling, and (5) **outbidding**. Of course, it is possible for groups to change their strategies over time or to utilize a combination of these basic strategies as part of their efforts to achieve their goals.

The **attrition strategy** is one that is designed to wear down the government and convince political leaders to change policies in a direction preferred by a terrorist organization. The attacks are intended to force the government to see that changes in policy will be easier than absorbing the damage created by the terrorist group. The costs of the terrorism can lead to the desired changes. A colony is granted its independence; discriminatory laws are repealed; immigration policies are changed. The attacks are likely to end if the necessary changes occur. Intimidation is directed toward the public as the key audience and its objective is to convince the population at large that the government is weak and can no longer protect important groups or society at large. The ultimate objective for undermining public support that is the key component of this strategy is usually the overthrow of the government, and perhaps a complete change in the political system as well. In these circumstances, the terrorist group is unlikely to end its campaign if the government simply changes policies.

Provocation is a more intermediate strategy and is basically designed to attempt to get the authorities to overreact. The terrorists are trying to goad the government or its security personnel into actions that will alienate a portion of the population. If the government can be induced into launching indiscriminate attacks against groups in society or arresting and detaining members of a religious, ethnic, economic, or ideological group, or limiting civil liberties for the society as a whole, the dissident organization may be able to attract additional supporters and at the same time weaken the government. When it works it can be a very effective means of attracting recruits and financial support if heavy-handed actions by the police or security forces alienate individuals or groups. This type of provocation can, of course, be combined with the other strategies. It can, for example, be a significant part of an attrition strategy designed to shift support from the government to the dissidents and can also complement an **intimidation strategy**.

Spoiling and outbidding are usually more intermediate strategies intended to strengthen an organization for a longer struggle or to avoid what the group sees as a negative situation. The **spoiling strategy** is frequently designed to prevent an outcome such as a truce or peace negotiations between the government and moderate opposition or some other group of violent dissidents. The terrorist group may believe that a truce or a peace settlement will permit a competing dissident group to gain power or that a settlement would undercut a long term objective by a premature end to the hostilities. The negotiated compromise thus becomes unacceptable because it would prevent ultimate victory. Attacks are launched to inflame the situation and to avoid such an outcome. Extremists on both sides of the Israeli-Palestinian conflict have used this technique to disrupt negotiations and undercut peace settlements at various times in that troubled area. Outbidding refers to efforts by competing groups to gain the allegiance of dissidents or others who are not satisfied with the current situation. Different organizations may be trying to appeal to the same segments of society or for assistance from abroad by appearing to be the most effective group opposing the government. The leaders of different dissident groups in these circumstances are acting in much the same fashion as politicians competing for votes or for control of many of the same resources. The groups will undertake attacks in an effort to attract recruits and financial support. In other cases groups may be seeking to retain their support base that is already present. Further, new attacks or a series of attacks could be used to convince supporters that the organization is still active and effective and the group should continue to receive support.

ROBBERIES

Finances are important for any terrorist organization. There are many ways that groups raise money for the cause (the Box below). The techniques include violent activities. One common method for raising funds is through bank robberies and similar actions. The robberies are designed to provide financing for the organizations; they are not undertaken for profit for a criminal gang or individual

Terrorist groups have developed a number of mechanisms for financing their operations including channeling money through charities and front organizations, buying gold and gems, drug trafficking, smuggling, and operating legitimate businesses. (Raphaeli 2003)

but to assist in the achievement of the ultimate political objectives. The robberies can also have the secondary benefit of increasing fear in the public and weakening support for the government if the police or security forces are unable to prevent these kinds of activities. The funds generated from the robberies, of course, can be used to purchase weapons and explosives or otherwise increase the potential of a group for continuing its struggle. **The Order** was a right-wing group in the United States that intended to change the government. While it lasted less than two years in the 1960s, it successfully robbed a series of banks and armored cars. It netted more than $4 million, most of which as never recovered (Michael 2003: 98). Other terrorist organizations rely on robberies and other types of criminal activity to finance their activities.

KIDNAPPINGS AND OTHER HOSTAGES

Many groups have resorted to kidnappings as a technique. Like robberies, kidnappings can serve multiple purposes. They demonstrate the abilities of the group to the government and the public, and they also indicate that the government is weak and that individuals in society are vulnerable. The individuals who are kidnapped may also be important symbols of the government, political groups, businesses, etc. Successfully kidnapping them indicates that the government cannot even protect its own personnel or supporters. Finally, kidnappings have proven to be a source of income for some groups when they receive ransoms for prominent individuals. The combination of funding, intimidation, and publicity has made kidnapping an effective tactic for many groups, and the success in one country seems to have encouraged other organizations to use it. Latin American groups in the 1970s and 1980s became quite adept at raising money and attention for their causes with such kidnappings. They have often targeted foreign executives of multinational corporations with investment in their countries. The multinational companies were ideal targets since they were often unpopular with many people, and they were willing to pay the ransoms.

Hostage situations have some similarities with kidnappings since the individual hostages are held against their will. Kidnappers, however, usually remain hidden from view whereas the hostage-taking is in public view. Unlike kidnappings where an individual is targeted, at least some of the hostages are likely to be individuals who happened to be in the wrong place at the wrong time. Hostage situations provide the terrorist groups with another opportunity to demonstrate the vulnerability of the government and to attract publicity for the goals of the organizations. Frequently, groups holding the hostages try to negotiate with the government for concessions and changes in policies. At the very least, groups holding the hostages can have political statements broadcast or published since few governments are willing to risk the deaths of hostages for refusing to publish a simple statement of grievances. Once the group starts to kill hostages, the publicity is likely to be present in any event. The dissident organizations at times have sought to gain the release of imprisoned comrades or others in jail. Such demands are both practical and symbolic because they would gain freedom for the individuals and at the same time demonstrate that the group can negotiate as an equal with a government. When they are successful in gaining the freedom of colleagues in prison, the loyalty of current members is increased. If the governments fail to negotiate, they risk seeing the hostages killed (unless the terrorists are bluffing) or will be forced to mount a rescue attempt which can lead to deaths among the hostages as well.

Hostage situations are more dangerous for the terrorist groups than kidnappings. If the kidnapping is well-planned, the members of the group involved do not become known to the police and are not placed in danger. Even a well-planned taking of hostages places the members of the organization in danger of death or capture. The potential costs of hostage situations are not just higher for the government. In October 2002 when Chechen dissidents seized a theater in Moscow with over 800 hostages, the Russian government eventually mounted a rescue operation. The rescue attempt was only a partial success. More than 100 of the hostages died in the rescue attempt, creating a great deal of negative publicity for the government. On the other hand, there were 40 to 50 dissidents who were also killed. There are many terrorist organizations that are too small to be able to afford these kinds of losses and even large organizations cannot continuously sustain such losses.

ASSAULTS

Terrorists will often assault individuals as a tactic without intending to kill the target. Assaults demonstrate that the individuals are vulnerable and send a broad warning to the target audience or audiences without the stigma of murdering anyone. The victim also remains alive as continuing proof of the abilities of the organization and the government's inability to prevent attacks. The attack itself can also generate publicity for the group. The Red Brigades in Italy developed the particularly effective technique of **kneecapping**. Members of the group would approach the victim and shoot him in one or both knees. This technique was especially effective since it required the assailant to get very close to the victim, demonstrating how vulnerable a person could be. The attackers would then get away providing evidence of the government's ineptitude and the ability of the dissidents. The Red Brigades opted to undertake the more difficult task of getting close to a victim rather than shooting him at a distance with a rifle or killing with a remotely detonated bomb since it demonstrated the abilities of the group. Because the Red Brigades at this stage were 'only' wounding the victims, even if they were likely to be crippled as a consequence of the attack, they avoided the negative publicity that would have come with killing them.

These kinds of assaults maximize the terror aspect of the dissidents because it appears that anyone can be attacked. It suggests that the government cannot protect people that are at risk. At one level, this conclusion is misleading since the terrorists have the advantage of choosing not to assault an individual who is too closely guarded. There is no doubt that the Red Brigades aborted some attempts at kneecapping because they could not get close to the individual initially chosen. In those cases, however, they could simply move on to a new target, and once he had been successfully assaulted, the perception was created that everyone was vulnerable and that the government was ineffective, a perception that was not necessarily correct but still effective in creating fear in the target audience. For the terrorists the perception of vulnerability, even if not exactly accurate, serves their purpose quite well.

HIJACKINGS

Hijacking has been one of the standard techniques used by terrorists (and others) around the world. Hijackings have been used as a means to generate publicity for many groups and their objectives. The more modern hijackings by their very nature usually include a large number of hostages. The hostages are frequently from more than one country creating opportunities for enhanced publicity. Planes are relatively easy to control with their confined spaces, and when – or if – terms are negotiated for the release of hostages in exchange for some concessions, a ready means of departure is available for the terrorists to a neutral country (where the hostages and plane can then be released). Hijackings were quite effective for a period of time until enhanced security measures began to limit opportunities for success. Even weak airport security can be a deterrent since any potential hijackers could be caught. Small groups cannot risk the capture of members for no benefits. The captured members of the group, furthermore, could become a liability in the hands of the security forces since they could identify other members of the organization, future plans, or key locations used by the group.

Terrorist groups have occasionally used the hijacking technique against other types of transportation targets, including trains, buses, and ships. The same principles apply in general to these targets, although buses and trains may be less likely to have passengers from many different countries. The terrorists will also have to arrange some means of escape, even when they are successful in getting some of their demands met and generating the publicity they are seeking. While trying to leave the country where the attack takes place, they could be vulnerable to attack or arrest. Ships provide a target that could generate media attention and include multinational passenger lists. They also can provide the necessary means of escape to a neutral country, if such an arrangement can

The first recorded hijacking occurred in 1930 in Peru when anti-government dissidents took over a small plane in order to drop propaganda leaflets over the capital. (Piszkiewicz 2003: 2)

be negotiated. The journey to a safe port, however, is likely to be a slow one providing opportunities for interception or action by special military forces. Ships also have the disadvantage in that a vessel of any size is going to be more difficult to effectively control for a small group of militants.

ASSASSINATION

Assassinations are another frequent tactic for terrorists. The victim of the assassination is not necessarily a particular individual chosen for elimination but rather a member of a particular group. An assassination designed to remove a specific individual to bring about political change is political murder but not necessarily terrorism. For example, the German officers who tried to kill Hitler desired a change in leadership, but Hitler had to be removed as an individual in order for this change to occur, and there was no intended target audience for the violence. A campaign of assassinations against members of a particular group, however, is a different situation. The goal of assassination as a form of terrorism is to spread terror among the broader group, which is the target audience for the violence. The anarchists wanted to bring about change in government policies by assassinating monarchs and other political leaders. They hoped that political leaders elsewhere would undertake the desired political reforms in order to avoid death. Larger terrorist groups are able to undertake such campaigns as part of the broader effort to intimidate the target audience and the broader public and as part of a strategy of attrition.

BOMBS

Explosives are involved in a great many terrorist actions. In fact, they are the most common form of terrorist activity, used in approximately half of all terrorist actions (Enders and Sandler 2006: 7). Of course, bombs come in many sizes, shapes, and levels of destructiveness. Most bombs are small, but some explosive devices, however, can cause much more damage. Bombs are a very flexible weapon for terrorists to use. They can be designed for assassinations, to cause casualties, to damage buildings, or for other purposes. They

> If a political leader is killed to permit someone else to assume
> power, that action is a political murder, it is not terrorism. If the
> leader is killed to send a message to other members of the ruling
> political elite, however, then the assassination is terrorism.
> (Schmid 1992: 10)

can be constructed from many different components. Letter bombs
cause less damage and are generally designed to kill or injure a
recipient. The improvised explosive devices (IEDs) used in Iraq
after 2003 and increasingly used in Afghanistan are examples of
how destructive such innovatively engineered devices can be. Car
bombs that have been used are almost always intended to destroy
buildings or cause a large number of casualties in most cases. The
technique of using car bombs with regular explosives or fertilizer
based bombs spread very quickly once it was demonstrated how
effective such devices could be. As a consequence, many different
groups began to use them. The knowledge of how to prepare the
bombs spread very quickly through the media and the internet, and
this knowledge is now generally available. The fact that fertilizer,
which is a major component of the bombs, can be relatively easily
purchased in many countries has made them more destructive. It
has also been a factor in the popularity of their use. Car bombs were
used against the federal office building in Oklahoma City and in the
first attempt to bring down the World Trade Center Towers. They
were also used by the IRA in its campaigns in Northern Ireland, and
they became a popular choice by dissidents throughout the Middle
East. More sophisticated bombs have been used against airliners
once it became more difficult to arrange hijackings. Groups willing
to detonate bombs on airliners are obviously willing to accept a
significant loss of life in the campaigns to achieve their objectives.

The September 11 attacks were another example of the use of
a special type of bomb in a new way. The four airliners that were
hijacked became sophisticated bombs used against buildings that
could not otherwise be reached. The Pentagon and White House (the
probable target of the airliner that crashed in Pennsylvania) were
particularly inaccessible to attacks in other ways. The attack was

quite well planned. The four planes were hijacked simultaneously and directed to their targets. All four flights were early flights, which limited the chance of airport delays. The United flight that crashed in Pennsylvania, however, left late, throwing this part of the attack off schedule and explaining its eventual failure. The four flights were all transcontinental flights, which meant they were carrying extra aviation fuel. The planes were hijacked on a Tuesday morning – a day when there would be fewer passengers on average, making the takeovers easier. The hijackers also relied on what had become standard operating procedures for the airliners, which called for the crews to cooperate with the hijackers in anticipation of political demands and the eventual release of planes, crews, and passengers. Of course, no one anticipated that this would be a new style of hijacking with a much deadlier purpose.

The 9/11 attacks were not the first attempts to use airliners as bombs. In 1995 Algerian dissidents hijacked an Air France flight with the apparent intent of crashing it into the Eiffel Tower. French commandos recaptured the plane in Marseille when it was on the ground for refueling, which threw that attempt into disarray. Israel shot down a Libyan airliner in the 1970s that had bypassed its destination in Cairo and strayed well off course and was flying over the Sinai Peninsula. The Israelis feared that the plane had been taken over and was going to be used against a target in Israel. They feared the same situation when they shot down a small plane from Lebanon near Tel Aviv in 2001 (Karmon 2002: 197). The potential for attacks with planes against targets in the United States or elsewhere probably should have been better anticipated by the authorities than it was.

It appears that Osama bin Laden did not expect the attacks to totally destroy the World Trade Center Towers. He seemed to want to cause major damage to the upper levels and cause significant casualties. The attacks were much more successful than that, of course, and he was pleased that the destruction exceeded expectations. (Robbins 2002: 357–8).

OTHER CONVENTIONAL WEAPONS

Some bombs qualify as conventional weapons while some others would fall into the category of unconventional. Terrorist organizations rely on all kinds of other conventional weapons. Whatever is available can be used. Tools, knives, handguns, shotguns, and rifles are rather common, especially when groups first appear. As groups become more organized and acquire more money (through contributions, external supporters, bank robberies, kidnappings, drugs, or other means), they can begin to gain access to more sophisticated weapons. Rifles with telescopic sights can become an important weapon for assassinations. Groups that persist and attract support may be able to get weapons from raids on police stations or by buying weapons from corrupt officials. As noted above, bombs can be made in all kinds of ways. Whether they are professionally made or improvised, they can be very deadly.

If they can, groups acquire more dangerous weapons when the opportunity presents itself. A variety of groups have been able to get their hands on surface to air missiles. There have been a number of attempts to use such weapons against civilian airliners, and rebels in the Sudan and Rhodesia have destroyed airliners with such weapons. Anti-tank weapons (rockets) are very effective against civilian vehicles, including ones that are armored and have bullet proof glass. Mortars or other forms of light artillery can be used for attacks when the terrorists cannot get close to the targets. One Palestinian group used motorized gliders to get an attack team inside Israel. This approach avoided the heavily patrolled land

The **17 November Organization** in Greece was a leftist group opposed to the regime in power. It needed weapons for a planned attack. Lacking alternative sources, members of the group went to the national war museum in Athens near closing time where they tied up the staff and a few visitors and stole World War II vintage weapons and ammunition. The stolen weapons were then used for the attack. (Corsun 1992: 110) border and the probability of radar detection present with other types of aircraft.

In general, terrorists can use any weapon that is available to the police, the security forces, or the military if they can get them. Many groups, in fact, do acquire weapons from these sources. Terrorist organizations have frequently demonstrated an ability to adapt a variety of things, some of them unlikely, into weapons. Not all the unusual weapons work as expected, but some of them have. Once a technique has proven to be successful, other groups elsewhere in the world will copy it. The internet has provided a mechanism for the rapid dissemination of information, including material on bomb building and other weapons. Some terrorist organizations have also looked into using more unconventional weapons.

WEAPONS OF MASS DISRUPTION

There has been increasing concern that terrorist groups will be able to take advantage of the complexity and the vulnerability of modern society in other ways. Much that goes on in modern society is dependent upon computer systems or other control systems that rely on computers. A hacker could penetrate a critical system – such as an air control system, a traffic control system for railroads or subways, the internet, a financial network, systems with medical records, or similar operations – and create havoc by planting a virus or dangerous instructions inside the system. Many different organizations and government agencies have had to deal with persons who have hacked into their systems in the past. To date, the computer hackers have generally been individuals having 'fun' by penetrating the systems. In a few cases, hackers have been interested in extorting money or stealing funds. While there does not appear to have been any terrorist successes in this area, there is the possibility of the danger of such disruptions in the future. At least some organizations have attracted persons with the necessary expertise, and it would be surprising if they had not at least considered some form of cyber attack or checked into the possibilities. If a successful computer attack were to occur on a critical system, the resulting disruption could generate significant problems and spread the fear that is the hallmark of terrorism.

WEAPONS OF MASS DESTRUCTION

A much greater fear for many than weapons of mass disruption is the potential use of weapons of mass destruction. Generally included in this category are chemical, biological, nuclear, and radiological weapons that are capable of killing large numbers of people if they are deployed. While it is possible that such weapons could be used in a more limited capacity, currently the greater fear is their potential for making large areas unlivable and for large death tolls.

An early and continuing fear has been that some group of terrorists would somehow acquire a nuclear weapon and use it or threaten to use it unless changes in policies, governments, or boundaries occurred. Even a tactical nuclear weapon that is designed to do limited damage would be a tremendous threat to a major city. There is no evidence that any terrorist organization has been able to acquire such a weapon, although some groups such as al Qaeda and Aum Shinriyko have tried. A well-financed group could attempt to build their own devices. The knowledge to build such a weapon is readily available, including information in libraries and on the internet. The difficulty is not in knowing how to build such a weapon but in getting enough weapons-grade materials to use in the bomb.

A much more likely possibility than the explosion of a nuclear weapon would be a radiological or **dirty bomb** in which the explosion of a conventional bomb would include radioactive materials that could contaminate the area where the explosion occurred. The initial explosion would cause damage and death, while the radioactive materials that were spread would then continue to cause illness and death to those exposed to the blast or those in the area in the immediate aftermath of the explosion. A dirty bomb could make an area uninhabitable or require major, specialized cleanup, compounding the economic damage done by the initial explosion. Some terrorist groups have considered using such dirty bombs but they have not yet done so. The threat is a real one, however, since acquiring radioactive material is much easier than getting weapons-grade nuclear material. If terrorists gained control of a nuclear power facility, they might have the opportunity to create the equivalent of a dirty bomb. The explosion at Chernobyl in what is now the Ukraine demonstrated how serious such an occurrence could be. Of course, security at nuclear facilities has been increased to prevent just such an event. The danger that a dirty bomb will be used remains real, and the threat seems more dangerous than any possibility of the use of a nuclear bomb.

Chemical weapons also have the potential to cause mass casualties. Chemical weapons were common in World War I, and they were used by Saddam Hussein in Iraq against domestic opponents and against the Iranian armed forces. The knowledge of how to make chemical weapons is readily available, although manufacturing such weapons with potent effects is more difficult. Aum Shinriyko in Japan did manufacture **sarin gas** (a nerve gas) and then used it in an attempt to cause mass casualties in the Tokyo subway system. The attack failed to achieve this result because the gas was not potent enough, even though thousands were hospitalized. The attack, moreover, got the full attention of the Japanese authorities resulting in the arrest of key members of the cult and a general weakening of the organization. (Aum Shinriyko still exists under a different leader, but no longer appears to be involved in violent activity. It is also highly probable that the authorities are keeping a very watchful eye on the group.)

This Japanese cult also tried to develop biological weapons but was not particularly successful. Other groups have also tried to develop such weapons but with little success. One recorded biological attack occurred late in 2001 in the United States when letters contaminated with anthrax were mailed to a variety of individuals in the media and politics. While only a few people died as a consequence of these mailings, the incident was quite successful in generating widespread fear. Part of the reason for the widespread panic was because it came so quickly after the 9/11 attacks. In addition, the biological nature of the attack made it more threatening. If the same number of people had been killed in a conventional bomb explosion, it would not have had the same impact. The use of a new type of weapon, however, had a much greater psychological effect. While the person or persons responsible has not been definitely identified, the initial fears that the attacks were another effort by al Qaeda was largely disproved since the anthrax strain in question originated in the

United States. It appears that the person responsible had a domestic agenda.

Biological and chemical attacks, like nuclear ones, are not very likely to be used in the immediate future. They all require significant financial resources and organizational capabilities. A successful chemical attack would require large quantities of the toxin that would have to be delivered under ideal conditions. A contagious biological weapon could easily get out of control. It is possible, however, to envision groups with a great antipathy to the West or to Muslims or to black Africans starting an epidemic in an area that contained a concentration of the target population. As a consequence, the use of biological weapons is a possibility in some circumstances for a group with enough money, organization, and intolerance to launch an attack. For the most part, the difficulties inherent with developing and using these weapons of mass destruction make their use much less likely than conventional weapons.

SUICIDE ATTACKS

A technique that has already been mentioned in other contexts is that of the suicide attack. It was used for the 9/11 attacks, against US marines and French paratroopers in Lebanon, against targets in Israel, by the Tamil Tigers with great regularity during their long struggle against the government of Sri Lanka, in Iraq and Afghanistan with great frequency against US forces and other foreign troops, and in many other countries and situations even if somewhat less often. These suicide attacks have been deadlier

There are significant practical difficulties involved with using exotic weapons such as biological or chemical agents; therefore, terrorists will often prefer the tried and true conventional weapons and techniques (Cameron 1999: 279). There is, of course, less chance of failure with the conventional techniques, and small groups often cannot risk failure that would come with the use of a new technique.

than most conventional attacks. In a suicide attack, the person with the bomb can detonate it at a time when casualties are likely to be the greatest. If in danger of being apprehended by security personnel there is a last opportunity to explode the device rather than letting it be disarmed. Suicide attacks can also demonstrate to observers as well as target audiences how determined the group is and how far it is willing to go to achieve its objectives. There is the implicit suggestion that such a level of determination will mean that the struggle is likely to last a long time. Compared to other types of attacks, suicide attacks are quite cost-effective for a terrorist organization (Dolnik and Bhattacharjee 2002). The group can usually find volunteers from its own ranks since involvement in a terrorist organization is inherently risky and casualties among activists involved in conventional (non-suicide) attacks can be high. The relatively low cost of suicide attacks and their effectiveness helps to explain why the technique has spread to new groups and new regions.

Suicide attacks may have the greatest potential for casualties if combined with weapons of mass destruction. Individuals willing to die in an attack could unleash an even more devastating attack. A volunteer could be injected with a contagious disease that could be spread by casual contact and sent out to infect as many people as possible in the target population before he or she died. Many of the difficulties of dealing with radiological or chemical materials, such as concern about being poisoned from dealing with them, would diminish if activists intended to die in an attack. A suicide attacker could always detonate explosive spreading chemical or radioactive elements if discovery or arrest were imminent. This potential combination of commitment and technology is a daunting prospect for the future.

FALSE FLAG ATTACKS

There is an additional tactic that can be used in conjunction with different weapons and different types of actions such as bombs or assassinations. In one type of **false flag attack** a group will undertake actions in the hope that an entirely different organization will be blamed for the action. For example, a right-wing group will plant bombs against targets that would typically be chosen by left-wing groups in order to get the government to crack down of the leftists. Similarly, a religious or ethnic group could pick targets that would lead the public and the authorities to blame a completely different segment of society. Governments might even use such false flag attacks to permit more stringent control of potential opposition groups. Shortly after coming to power, Adolf Hitler used a fire in the German parliament to ban the German communist party. The fire was most likely started on Hitler's orders with just such a goal in mind. It is not surprising that conspiracy theories have appeared to suggest that the CIA or Israel were responsible for the 9/11 attacks in order to accomplish other goals by driving a wedge between the West and Islamic countries and populations.

Another type of false flag (or false front) attack occurs when a terrorist group will claim credit for an attack under a different name. In this fashion the new group may bear the blame for any unnecessary casualties or for other unpopular or otherwise negative consequences. In this fashion an attrition or **provocation strategy** can be continued against the government without the known dissident group running the risk of decreased support. Some times previously unheard of groups claim responsibility for one or two attacks, and then the groups disappear. Some of these examples no doubt reflect the use of personnel from the existing organization to launch the attack in order to observe the reactions of the government and the public while still avoiding the possible negative consequences of new types of attacks.

ESCALATION

One very real possibility with terrorist organizations is the prospect that there will be escalation in terms of techniques and the damage done and casualties inflicted. When the initial types of attacks do not accomplish the objectives that the group is seeking, there are two choices assuming the group has not been detected and dealt with by the security forces or the police. First, it is possible that the group will give up the effort and disappear if they are not willing to take the chance on killing people. Such demobilization of the members might involve voluntary exile if it is not safe to remain in their own country. The second alternative is to escalate the level of violence – from kidnappings and assault to assassination and murder, from attacks with limited casualties to those with great death tolls, from conventional attacks to suicide attacks, even from attacks with conventional weapons to more exotic weapons or weapons designed to cause mass casualties. While not all groups can survive to consider escalation, some that do are likely to become involved in patterns of escalation. Most members of these groups are committed enough to their cause to engage in illegal and violent activities. As escalation begins to happen, it becomes even more difficult for these committed members to turn back. Opportunists and criminals might drop away with escalation, but they are not the core of the group to begin with. The committed will persist in their efforts to bring about change.

CONCLUSIONS

The techniques discussed above, which are potentially available to all terrorist groups are quite varied. Like terrorism itself, these tactics are not defined by the underlying motivation of the organizations or their basic objectives. While most groups use whatever weapons that they can acquire, some organizations will be unwilling to use suicide attacks or mount actions that will lead to large numbers of casualties. The decision not to cause casualties is often done for tactical or strategic reasons. If the group is seeking popular support and the public in question would be turned away by mass casualties, then such attacks will not occur. If members of the support population and the general population are intermingled rather than segregated, then car bombs and similar tactics would be counterproductive. If, however, the ethnic, class, or religious group is separated from the rest of the population, such attacks become more likely. While there are very real and important differences in the willingness of organizations to cause death, all terrorist groups by definition are willing to use violence, and most are willing to accept the possibility of at least limited casualties. Many groups that start out trying to avoid hurting people by focusing on symbolic attacks or kidnapping, however, often do eventually escalate to more violent behavior. If they decide to escalate, there are plenty of proven techniques available for them to use.

KEY TERMS

anthrax, attrition strategy, Aum Shinrikyo, dirty bomb, false flag attacks, intimidation strategy, kneecapping, the Order, outbidding strategy, provocation strategy, Red Brigades, sarin gas, 17 November Organization, spoiling strategy

FURTHER READING

Dolnik, A. (2008), "13 Years since Tokyo: Re-Visiting the 'Superterrorism' Debate," *Perspectives on Terrorism*, 2, 2: 3–11.

Dolnik provides a useful discussion of the likelihood of the use of weapons of mass destruction in the future.

Dolnik, A. and R. Gunaratna (2006), "Dagger and Sarin: The Evolution of Terrorist Weapons and Tactics," in A. T. H. Tan (ed.), *The Politics of Terrorism*, London: Routledge, 25–39.

This chapter summarizes the wide range of weapons used by terrorists over time.

O'Neil, A. (2003) "Terrorist Use of Weapons of Mass Destruction: How Serious Is the Threat?" *Australian Journal of International Affairs*, 57, 1: 99–112.

O'Neil suggests that the likelihood of any use of weapons of mass destruction by terrorists is very small, but there will always be a danger of such use.

Pape, R. A (2005) *Dying to Win: The Logic of Suicide Terrorism*. New York: Random House.

Pape's work has become a classic in terms of discussing suicide bombing. He argues, however, that virtually all such attacks are related to nationalist issues and not religious ones. It appears that he stretches the definition of nationalist or territorial issues to make this point.

Tucker, J. B. (ed.), *Toxic Terror: Assessing Terrorist Use of Chemical and Biological Weapons*, Cambridge, MA: MIT Press.

The selections in this collection deal with various attempts to use chemical and biological weapons. The book provides an excellent background on the difficulty of using chemical and biological agents since the vast majority of attempts failed completely.

WHO ARE THE TARGETS?

The wide variety of techniques available to terrorist groups was discussed in the previous chapter. These techniques can be used against different targets, and no technique is unique to a particular type of target. The persons responsible for the attacks may seek to maximize property damage or cause casualties. The targets of the violence may be chosen because they have symbolic or shock value (Stern and Midi 2008: 29). Frequently a government is the underlying target for dissident organizations because of its leadership, policies, institutions, or state boundaries. The targets, moreover, can include property, the general public, some portion of the population, or specific groups of individuals. The target audiences and those chosen for the attacks usually are chosen because of their relationship to the government, but in some cases the target audiences reflect the agendas of other groups in society. The target audiences of government terrorism are generally similar, but there are some important differences with this type of terrorism.

PROPERTY ATTACKS

A majority of attacks are solely property attacks directed against buildings, monuments, offices, or other physical structures related to some of the groups and situations described below. The property attacks are designed to gain attention for the demands and goals of the groups and to demonstrate the weaknesses of the government and its inability to provide protection. It sends a message to the target audience as well and frequently contains the implicit threat that there will be actions designed to kill or wound people if the demands for change are not met.

While some terrorist groups start with property attacks and escalate to attacks on people, many never progress to endangering people. Environmental groups and animal rights groups, for example, have tended to focus actions on the property of the universities, corporations, and other businesses that damage the environment or mistreat animals. They have chosen operations of companies involved in activities such as logging, animal testing, the fur business, and similar activities or companies that generate large amounts of pollution, which are considered unacceptable. These groups have caused millions of dollars of damage in the countries where they have operated. These attacks have been very effective in many cases and changes have occurred since the attacks have harmed the economic bottom line of the companies or universities. Companies and universities have had to pay more for enhanced security in addition to facing adverse publicity when the actions have led to increased media attention to their operations. Most terrorist organizations, however, are less effective with a reliance on property attacks since the changes they desire are political rather than economic.

GOVERNMENT OFFICIALS

Government officials have become a frequent target of dissident groups. They may be assaulted, kidnapped, or killed. The officials chosen may be specific to a particular ministry or government function. Police officers and judges often become targets because they are clear representatives of the authority of the government and are often seen as part of the 'corrupt' criminal justice system. Mayors and district leaders can become targets for much the same reason. Those involved in the collection of taxes may be chosen since they can be very unpopular, and, thus, attacks against them can generate positive feelings for the terrorists in the general population. It is possible that virtually any one employed by the government can become a target, including postal workers, teachers, low-level bureaucrats, and any others. These bureaucrats serve as symbols of the government. Only larger dissident groups are likely to have the personnel to target the whole range of government employees. Smaller groups, or groups that start out small, will be more selective in choosing the officials they will attack. Members of the military and security can be targets as well, especially if they are off-duty and more vulnerable.

The victims of the attacks can be any member of the groups in question. The audience is usually all others in the same category as the victims – or all government employees – who may become future victims themselves. They are being warned about the dangers of being so directly involved in the activities of the government in power. A second audience frequently will include the general public who become aware of how weak the government is when it cannot even protect its own employees. If the government does appear weak in this regard, public support may decline. Government employees may become so concerned about their own safety that they become less effective. The government may also be forced to divert resources to protecting bureaucrats that would otherwise be used to catch the dissidents. This diversion of resources could provide an important tactical advantage to the terrorists.

A clear example of how effective such attacks can be is provided by the attacks in Iraq after 2003 on police and military recruiting centers. Many of the attacks have involved suicide bombers while others have relied on more conventional explosives that are detonated in the areas where potential recruits gather. All of these attacks have sent the clear message that even considering serving the government in a security capacity is dangerous. No doubt many potential recruits changed their plans as a result. In this case the attacks also had a very practical objective. If the government cannot find police or military recruits, then it will be more difficult for the government to defend itself. The attacks also provided a demonstration of the weakness of the government to the Iraqi public, since the government could not even provide protection at its own policy and military recruiting stations.

GOVERNMENT SUPPORTERS

The attention of dissident groups can extend beyond those directly involved in the government. Rallies by government supporters can be chosen for attacks as can pro-regime party workers. Newspapers and journalists supporting the government can become targets. Even media organizations that may not be pro-government, but which are critical of the terrorists or their goals may be chosen on the assumption that those not with the terrorist groups are against it. Organizations, whether business, labor, or professional as well as individuals seen as being pro-government, can be added to the list of those who will be targeted because of their support.

Attacks can be extended to include virtually any group that supports the government or its policies. Areas of the country or a city known for its positive view of the government may become the scene of car bombings or other bombs. Persons attending public ceremonies, parades, or patriotic celebrations could be put at risk by their simple presence at these events. Successful attacks of this type would demonstrate the weakness of the government due to its inability to protect its own supporters. Further, if public support becomes less obvious due to fear, the terrorist group will have gained an advantage in its ongoing confrontation with the government. Even the perception of declining support can have a negative effect on the government's ability to deal with terrorist threats as members of the public will no longer provide information or provide support in other ways.

RELIGIOUS TARGETS

If dissident terrorists have objectives rooted in particular religious views, then it is possible for other religious groups to become targets for violence. If the government is based on a majority or minority religious group and enforces policies favorable to that group at the expense of the dissidents, then not only the government and its officials but any member of the religion can become a target. All members of the group are assumed to be supporters of the government. The dissidents may target those of a different religious tradition as with Muslim versus Christian or the violence can occur within the same religious tradition as is the case with Protestants and Catholics or Sunni and Shia Muslims. Temples, mosques, and other places of worship can become symbolic property targets for this type of violence, and when property attacks or attacks against people occur at a place of worship, the logic behind the targeting is obvious. A cult like Aum Shinrikyo in Japan may simply target anyone who is not a member of the group providing the broadest target group of all.

At times the terrorism can be based in broader communities and will not necessarily involve direct attacks on governments.

The violence that occurred with the partition of British India into Pakistan and India represented terrorism and ethnic cleansing. The local majorities – Hindu and Muslim alike – attacked members of the minority religious community. They were often quite successful in driving out the minority group. There have been periodic clashes between Muslims and Hindus in India in the years that have followed. In Indonesia and the Philippines there has been violence and terrorism between Muslims and Christians that have occurred without directly involving the government.

There is one additional choice of targets that is in effect determined by religious views. Extremists of any religious tradition may target any group they see as overtly too secular. A wide variety of groups have been opposed to what they see as the spread of secular humanism, which they consider a great danger. For example, at times Osama bin Laden has been more concerned about the dangers of Western secularism than Western Christianity. Ironically, some extremist Christian groups in the United States share exactly the same fear. They frequently refer to the need to fight the ideas associated with secular humanism since they see these ideas as a threat to religious values. Another example would be the groups willing to use violence and terror to end abortion in the United States. These groups are in basic disagreement with policies that they see as a reflection of secular values. The anti-abortion movement in both its violent and its non-violent versions is rather unique in that it brings together persons of different religions who otherwise have very little in common theologically.

ETHNICITY

Members of particular ethnic groups, just like members of religious groups, can become targets for terrorist violence if they are facing a dissident group with ethnic or nationalist goals. Ethnicity defines members of the group as government supporters or so linked to the government that attacks against them is an attack against the government. During the struggle for independence in Algeria, the European settler population (which overwhelmingly opposed independence) became a target for terrorist attacks. The

> Members of extreme Islamic groups, like other violent
> fundamentalist religious groups, see themselves as part of a
> "cosmic struggle" with the antithetical forces represented by
> secularism. (Pillar 2001: 65)

violence in Darfur in the Sudan has involved groups with different ethnic identities. The Albanian dissidents in Kosovo targeted the minority Serbian population during their struggles with the central government since these Serbs were considered, usually correctly, as supporters of the central government. When there are problems between majority and minority ethnic groups, one group (or both) may target members of the other group in an effort to instill fear in order to achieve political objectives.

Attacks against members of specific ethnic groups are intended to raise the costs for the government and to generate public pressure from within the targeted groups for changes in government policies. Attacks against groups can also occur independently of the government. Extreme right-wing groups in Europe have attacked foreign refugees, guest workers, and others they consider outsiders in an effort to scare them away. Gypsies in Eastern Europe have also frequently become targets for violence that is designed to drive them away. Attacks against black Americans by the Ku Klux Klan and other white supremacist groups in the United States are also examples of ethnic targeting.

ENTIRE POPULATIONS

There can be times when the entire population of a country can become targets. Terrorist groups will attempt to use fear to have the public force their government to make changes in keeping with the objectives of the organization. These kinds of situations could develop in anti-colonial situations where groups seeking independence may try to inspire fear in the population of the colonial power in order to gain independence. The IRA, for example, launched bombing campaigns in England at various times as part of an effort to convince the British government to change its policies and to leave Northern Ireland. Various Palestinian groups have launched campaigns against Israeli citizens in general in what they see as an essentially anti-colonial struggle. In both these cases and others the dissident groups are trying to convince the public, and therefore the government, that keeping the colony is not worth the cost.

Many of those involved in the global jihad movement see themselves as engaged in a worldwide anti-colonial struggle against Western political, economic, and cultural domination of Islamic states, especially those in the Middle East. The entire populations of Western countries are often seen as the enemy. The entire populations share the guilt of their governments since they have supported government policies when they have attacked Islam. Campaigns based on strategies of attrition and intimidation are designed to force changes favorable to the objectives of those supporting the global jihad, including al Qaeda.

DOMESTIC ECONOMIC TARGETS

Some groups have focused on domestic economic targets in their efforts to win their political objectives. The animal rights groups and environmental groups usually choose business or university targets because they wanted them to change their practices. Other terrorist groups, however, target businesses as part of an effort to influence governments. Some of the attacks may be just against property while others may involve an intention to cause casualties. There are economic activities that have a fairly direct connection to governments as would be the case with national airlines or government corporations, and they become symbols of the government. In other situations, economic activities are targeted to display the weakness of the government. Utility lines and power stations may be destroyed to indicate this weakness and to demonstrate that society as a whole is vulnerable. More generally, many economic activities may be targets as part of a broader economic assault on the ability of the government to collect taxes and raise revenue. If important economic activities are disrupted, the government will lose tax revenues or royalty payments. The loss of revenue will then mean that the government has fewer resources available for all purposes. Diminished resources would reduce funds available for police or security forces, and there would be reductions in money available for programs that could address issues raised by the dissidents or to deal with issues that generate popular support for the dissidents. Reducing money available for highways, education, clean water supplies, agricultural programs, etc., could be even more effective for the dissident group than assassinating teachers or other government officials.

The economic rationale of this type of targeting can extend to efforts to discourage investment. Domestic investors who might provide employment and revenues may become targets in terms of their business activities or even as individuals. If the terrorist group can force domestic capital to flee and aggravate national economic problems, the government could then become more vulnerable. Foreign investors can become targets for these types of attacks for the same reasons. Campaigns of violence are designed to persuade the foreign investor to pull out of a country and look elsewhere. Even if existing foreign investment cannot be driven out, new investors may be put off by the danger and chose to invest elsewhere. Foreign investors, their plants, or other economic activities provide an additional advantage as targets. It is frequently the case that these investors are seen as draining local economies and taking advantage of the local population. As a consequence, they can be a very popular target with some segments of the domestic population, generating goodwill for the dissident group. Left-wing terrorist groups generally adhere to this view of foreign investment, and they see the multinational corporations as part of a global capitalist system that exploits and dominates both people and countries. Thus, foreign investors have a heightened symbolic value for these groups.

Groups have attacked foreign aid operations for similar reasons. If they are successful in providing help to the general public, the government is likely to experience increased popularity. If the foreign aid is providing necessary infrastructure or assistance for important economic activities, employment and revenues may go up. Successful foreign aid operations can thus strengthen the government and provide resources that potentially make the government more popular. The availability of aid may thus weaken

Carlos Marighella was a Brazilian leftist who authored the *Mini-Manual of the Urban Guerrilla*. This handbook was widely read by leftist terrorist groups that were willing to resort to violence. He advocated attacking both domestic and foreign investment as one way to weaken the state and to bring about a leftist takeover of the political system. (Laqueur 1977: 185)

the appeal of dissident groups with claims about government failure. If the aid agencies can be driven out, however, one source of potentially important support for the government will have been eliminated.

Petroleum pipelines and facilities have become favorite targets for economic attacks. Such facilities are frequently important for a national economy, and they are either government owned or foreign owned, therefore providing a symbolic element in addition to the economic damage that can be done. The various groups opposed to the US presence in Iraq after 2003 and the government that it supports have attacked these kinds of facilities with great regularity as part of an attempt to interrupt revenue flows to the government. Pipelines in particular are vulnerable to attack since it is difficult to effectively guard them and they are easy to disrupt. Pipelines can actually be repaired rather easily, but the constant disruption can be effective, especially if it discourages additional investment and strengthens popular doubts about the abilities of the government.

TOURISM

Tourists have come under special threat from many terrorist groups. In a number of countries, tourist revenues are quite important for the economy and jobs; the revenues also provide tax resources and scarce foreign currency. Efforts to undercut the tourist trade have become part of an economic assault intended to eliminate these resources. If the tourists are driven away, the government can face major problems. The inability of the government to deal with the threat also makes the authorities appear to be weak. Tourists as targets are also a vulnerable target since they are difficult to protect unless extreme, and costly, measures are adopted and these measures themselves would probably drive away the visitors as well.

In some circumstances foreign tourists can also be symbolic targets. Western tourists can be symbolic of the intrusion of external values, including secular values, into more traditional societies, including Islamic ones. The tourists themselves are likely to behave in ways that are contrary to local norms – the consumption of alcohol, choice of foods, women being inappropriately dressed, etc. A group can see an attack on the tourists as a way of protecting the traditional culture and local values from outside contamination. These kinds of attacks may have a certain appeal to at least portions of domestic populations which share these concerns about the intrusion of foreign ideas and values that threaten the local society.

The attack on tourists in Bali in Indonesia by Islamic extremists in 2002 illustrate how an action can be chosen for more than one reason and have more than one target audience. The attack clearly was designed to reveal the continuing vulnerability of the West. The tourists themselves were a symbolic target, a symbolism that was enhanced by the fact that the bombs went off in an area of nightclubs and bars. The attack also stuck at the Indonesian economy and created difficulties for the new democratic system that had replaced the previous military regime. Many of the more extreme Islamic groups have seen the newly elected democratic government as not being Islamic enough. A weakened government could provide opportunities for Islamic political groups of all kinds to increase their influence and to implement the appropriate policies. The attack was also staged in one of the few Hindu areas of the country, thus minimizing the potential for death of local Muslims (Lutz and Lutz 2008: 38). The attacks, consequently, had the potential of achieving a variety of objectives. The attacks that occurred in 2005 in Bali just as the tourism industry was beginning to recover from the 2002 attack was intended to continue to target the economic base of the Indonesian government and in addition to continue to strike against the West.

FOREIGN INTERESTS

Attacks against tourists, foreign aid agencies, and foreign investments are by their nature attacks against foreign interests. Foreign interests can be targeted in other ways. Activities associated with foreign countries and governments can become targets for other reasons. A foreign government may be supporting the domestic government that the dissidents oppose. Attacks against businesses, embassies, diplomatic personnel, students and professors, and others from the external country in question can be intended to send a message that the group wants a change in the foreign policy of the country. The intent is to mobilize public opinion in the foreign country to change policies. One of al Qaeda's stated goals is to force the United States and its allies to stop supporting governments in the Middle East that are authoritarian and which do not sufficiently follow Islamic principles in how Muslim states are governed.

While dissident groups may target foreign interests in their own country in an effort to change foreign policies, they may also go after these interests abroad. The attacks against the US embassies in Kenya and Tanzania in 1998 were part of an attempt to get the United States to modify its policies in the Middle East. Embassies make excellent targets for groups wishing to communicate messages to foreign governments while having the potential to embarrass the domestic government that cannot protect these facilities. Algerian extremists in the 1990s attacked French interests in Algeria because France was supporting the government in power, but they also set off a series of bombs in France to demonstrate their disagreement with the French government's policy of supporting the exiting Algerian government. The hijacking of the Air France flight with the intent to crash the plane into Paris was part of this effort to bring about policy changes. The end result is that foreign interests in general or those associated with a specific country can become targets as part of a broad campaign designed to weaken external support and assistance for a domestic government.

OTHER DISSIDENT GROUPS

Terrorist organizations may at times attack other dissident groups. As noted in Chapter 4 in the discussion of strategies, moderates may be considered dangerous to the objectives of the group as is the government. In some cases extremist groups will be competing for support, money and recruits with each other. The different dissident groups may attempt to outbid each other in efforts to gain recruits or financial supporters. In other situations, however, the competition may escalate and the different organizations may attack each other in an effort to eliminate rivals. On the one hand, such attacks do not always qualify as terrorism since they are essentially a very practical effort to eliminate a rival political group. The attacks, however, do send a message to any one in a target audience who might be considering forming or supporting a rival organization that it could be quite dangerous to do so.

VULNERABILITY OF TARGETS

Vulnerability will affect which individuals become victims within a targeted group, but it may also affect which groups a terrorist organization will choose. If journalists can be killed with greater ease than teachers, then journalists can become the victims to send a message to the target audience. If elected politicians are easier to reach than judges, then the politicians will serve as the victims. If the local Coca-Cola distributor is too difficult to target as a symbol of American presence in a foreign country, then the local McDonalds or Pizza Hut can serve just as well. One advantage that terrorist organizations frequently have is that they operate in a target rich environment where they have many options. It often appears to the public that terrorists have successfully struck, even though they may actually have been unable to go after their first or second choice of targets. Terrorist groups, of course, do not normally advertise their failures, so it is impossible to know of plans that failed unless some members of the group are actually caught or bombs are discovered and disarmed before they explode. Even failures can be made to appear as successes. If a bomb smuggled into a government building goes off prematurely at 2:00 a.m., the group can simply state that the bomb was intended to detonate at this time as a warning to the public while avoiding casualties and that next time a bomb will explode when people are present. Even a bomb that fails to explode can be claimed as a warning, especially if it was smuggled into a supposedly secure building.

It was noted in Chapter 2 that certain countries are perhaps more vulnerable to terrorist activities than others. The civil liberties inherent in democratic systems have been seen as making these political systems more vulnerable because terrorists can operate more freely. These vulnerabilities appear to permit foreign dissidents to attack targets associated with their home government on the soil of democratic states. Weak states almost by definition provide many opportunities. They can invite campaigns by domestic dissidents seeking changes. They can also provide appropriate sites for third-party attacks. The choice of Kenya and Tanzania for attacks against the US embassies in part reflected the relatively weak counterintelligence capabilities and limited security forces of these two countries (at least in terms of detecting foreign threats). These two US embassies were more vulnerable in these countries than US embassies in some other countries.

A final category of states that are likely to be vulnerable are political systems that are in transition. Political systems moving from a more authoritarian regime to a more open, democratic society can be especially vulnerable. Such new governments are unlikely to have kept the security forces or secret police that served the old governments since such agencies would be of doubtful loyalty and compromised by their activities under authoritarian rulers. As a

Latin American leftist groups in the 1970s staged a number of successful embassy takeovers as part of their campaigns to overthrow existing governments. They initially selected the embassies of major countries, particularly the United States, for these actions. When these countries upgraded the security at their embassies, the dissident groups simply chose the more vulnerable embassies of smaller countries (Jenkins 1981: 21). The choice of targets was obviously influenced by defensive measures that were taken, but the groups were able to continue to be successful by simply changing their targets.

consequence, the ability to detect and oppose terrorist activities will be weaker for at least a period of time. Indonesia was in the early years of a transition to a democratic system at the time of the Bali bombing in 2002, and the security apparatus of the military regime had been partially dismantled. Even if a political system is changing from one type of authoritarian system to another, there may still be a period of vulnerability if the security forces are in disarray due to changes in leadership and personnel. The new Islamist regime that came to power in Iran after the overthrow of the Shah in 1979 had to deal with a campaign by leftist and secular groups. The new government was vulnerable at first since the security agencies inherited from the Shah had been purged of their personnel. The regime had to build new security forces to deal with the dissidents.

GOVERNMENT TERRORISM AGAINST CITIZENS

While a great deal of terrorist activity is by dissidents and directed against governments, there are cases where governments will tolerate or accept attacks against groups of their own citizens that they consider disloyal, threatening, or otherwise a problem. The government may be indirectly supportive of attacks against particular groups or more actively involved in the terrorism. In cases of more direct activity, government personnel may participate in the assaults on target populations. The government involvement in this type of activity becomes terrorism instead of repression when members of the target groups become the victims of the attacks to instill fear in a broader group (see the Box below). The broader group that is the target audience for the terrorism may be

> There is a difference between government repression or oppression and terrorism. If citizens can avoid arrest, torture, prison, and death by following the rules of the state, however bad these rules might be, the state may be repressive but it is not practicing terrorism. When individuals can become victims to send a message to other members of the group, then they are victims of terrorism (Sproat 1991: 24).

chosen because of ethnicity or race, religious beliefs, class-based, regional, or ideological. The victims for the violence are random individuals from within the broader groups who serve as a means of spreading fear to the other members of the group.

There have been cases where governments have tolerated actions by groups to silence opposition or control groups inside the state. Authorities in the area around Mumbai (Bombay) in India have stood aside when the local Muslim population has been attacked by Hindu activists, and there have been few if any cases of anyone involved in the violence ever being charged (let convicted) because of the violence. Fascist parties in Europe between World War I and World War II often had the tacit support of their governments when they attacked socialists and communists. White supremacist groups in the American south for many years were able to attack black Americans with relative impunity since the local governments usually never charged anyone with the crimes.

Government agencies can move toward more active support of attacks against its citizens by domestic groups. The government is already providing benefits to them since they do not need to worry about being arrested or evading the security forces. The government can provide finance, arms, and training for groups, such as party militias or paramilitary organizations, which are involved in the terrorism. Government officials might even provide information on possible targets for the group members. The organizations receiving the support are thus much more effective in launching their attacks. In the most extreme cases, the government may organize unofficial **death squads** that kill members of the target groups. These death squads often involve members of the police, security forces, or the military, but they are not technically operating under government orders. The attacks against members of the target audience are designed to silence opposition to the government, eliminate political trends that are considered threatening or undesirable, or even to force the target population to migrate. In all of these cases the terrorism can be much more deadly because of the support given by the government.

The resort to irregular means of control by the government is inevitably a sign of weakness on the part of the authorities.

A government that is firmly in control and strong enough has sufficient security forces, secret police, and other mechanisms for dealing with threats and does not have to rely on terrorism. These governments can rely on fear of arrest for specific offenses or for challenging the system. Weaker governments, however, may rely on such activities by their supporters. In some cases a government may be unable to prevent violence among groups and choose to support the groups that are seen as more loyal. In other cases, however, the government may lack the means for repression and choose to rely on irregular forces to undertake attacks. The government of Sudan first used pro-government militias in the civil war in the south in the 1980s and 1990s and more recently has used similar militias in Darfur in the western part of the country to deal with domestic groups opposed to the present government. In both cases the regular military forces could not control the situation on their own. At other times a government may be concerned about domestic or foreign public opinion and thus avoid using regular government forces in order to maintain plausible deniability for any involvement. This approach gives foreign governments the opportunity to avoid condemnations or negative actions since the problem is officially between domestic groups. In Nazi Germany, the first attacks against the Jewish population were not by official security forces but by paramilitary groups. Many foreign governments accepted the explanation that these assaults were due to domestic conditions and beyond the control of the regime.

CONCLUSIONS

Terrorist organizations can attack a wide range of targets. Many attacks are directed against property and not intended to cause casualties. The building or objects chosen have symbolic value, but the attacks also hold the implicit or explicit threat of escalation if political changes are not forthcoming. Many different portions of the population can become targets for either dissident or government terrorism. Some terrorist groups may even target the entire population of a country as has occurred with attacks by global jihadists opposed to events or Western support for secular governments in the Middle East or countries with Muslim populations. Domestic governments (as opposed to foreign occupation forces) are unlikely to target the entire population of their citizens since there are at least some privileged groups in society that support them. The targeting of members within particular groups is what has often given terrorism the appearance of randomness, but the victims are only random within groups since any member can serve to send the desired message of vulnerability to the target audience. Government tolerated or supported terrorism is often quite effective and can involve more casualties since the attackers do not have to worry about arrest or interference by the security forces.

KEY TERMS
death squads

FURTHER READING

Campbell, B. D. and A. D. Brenner (eds.), (2000) *Death Squads in Global Perspective: Murder with Deniability*, New York: St. Martin's.

The chapters in this book provide both a general background to the use of death squads and specific examples from many parts of the world.

Drake, C. J. M. (1998) "The Role of Ideology in Terrorists' Target Selection," *Terrorism and Political Violence*, 10, 2: 53–85.

This article provides examples on how ideology affects the choice of targets. It also provides more general views on the importance of target choice.

Lutz, J. M. and B. J. Lutz (2006) "Terrorism as Economic Warfare," *Global Economy Journal*, 6, 2: 1–20.

This article discusses how a variety of organizations in different countries have chosen economic targets as part of their strategies to weaken the governments that they are attacking.

6

WHO SUPPORTS TERRORISTS?

Terrorist organizations do not exist in a vacuum. They need to have some sources of support in order to survive for more than a brief period. Dissident terrorist groups need money and a flow of recruits in order to continue their struggle against governments, which usually have greater resources. Many dissident organizations fail quickly precisely because they cannot mobilize enough support, although they can fail for other reasons. Terrorist groups that have succeeded in surviving long enough to mount serious campaigns of actions against governments or other target groups, have been able to draw upon important sources of support – either domestic, foreign, or both. Governments that provide assistance to groups involved in terrorism against its own citizens, of course, do not usually have a problem in terms of resources. While these governments may be too weak to successfully use repression against the targeted groups, they can provide major support to paramilitary groups, militias, or vigilantes. The effects of such government support were discussed in Chapter 5, and groups receiving this support have a big advantage, and, as a consequence, do not usually rely on the other sources of support discussed below.

DOMESTIC SYMPATHIZERS

Most terrorist groups have specific objectives that they hope to achieve in their own country, and they are essentially domestic political organizations that are attempting to mobilize support from within their own country. Even the best of governments cannot please every group in society, and, consequently, there will be dissatisfaction with some of the policies in place. Governments that rely on repression obviously create the potential for opposition groups to develop within their own societies. Groups that are then able to organize in opposition to the government and survive can draw upon at least the tacit support of a portion of the population dissatisfied with the repression. At the very least, a portion of the population may be unwilling to provide information to the authorities or security forces, providing the terrorists with an obvious advantage. If the terrorists can launch some successful attacks, they may then be able to gain more active support. If these attacks weaken the government or demonstrate the inability of the government to protect citizens or supporters, the group may be able to mobilize even more adherents, even if some of the new supporters are opportunists rather than idealists committed to the cause.

Organizations rooted in ethnic or religious views have some advantages in appealing for support because they have a natural affinity with the members of the group. Domestic support for dissident groups in some circumstances can therefore be quite substantial. Palestinian groups in the West Bank and the Gaza Strip, for example, have often operated relatively openly. The population implicitly supports these groups in their resistance to Israel, and they provide very little information to the Israeli authorities. Persons who might be willing to provide information to the authorities face the prospect of retaliation if they are caught or even suspected of collaboration. Anti-colonial movements elsewhere in the world frequently have had similar levels of support. Other organizations will be more selective in mobilizing support by the nature of their objectives. Ideological groups have to depend upon persons sharing their views or make an effort to convert additional individuals to their cause. They are less likely to be able to mobilize support as readily as ethnic or religious groups.

Assistance can go beyond the tacit support of part or even all of the population. The group will need recruits for its attacks and individuals to provide safe houses and to collect intelligence for the organization. Domestic support can also include financial contributions that provide funds for weapons to meet the upkeep of activists involved in the actual attacks. The money can be especially important for groups that cannot raise funds from robberies or kidnappings. The Italian Red Brigades were fortunate early on in their history. One of their members inherited his father's

> Terrorist groups "generally cannot survive without either active or passive support from a surrounding population. Active support includes hiding members, raising money, providing other sustenance, and, especially, joining the organization. Passive support, as the phrase implies, is more diffuse and includes ignoring obvious signs of terrorist group activity, declining to cooperate with police investigations, sending money to organizations that act as fronts for the group, and expressing support for the group's objectives." (Cronin 2009: 104–5)

substantial fortune, and he used it to help fund the activities of the organization until he died. In other cases groups have relied on small contributions from their supporters or on family and friends.

FOREIGN GOVERNMENTS

When terrorist groups are present in a country, foreign governments are frequently blamed for the resulting violence. Some terrorist groups have actually been able to receive foreign support, including money, equipment – including arms and explosives, and training. This support from foreign governments can also include the use of diplomatic pouches for communications or simply allowing the groups to operate unhindered on their territory. Such safe havens can be very important for a group by providing secure locations for planning operations and opportunities for resting and recovering between operations without fear of arrest.

Foreign governments have often taken advantage of the existence of domestic groups in other countries to weaken a state that they consider threatening. During the Cold War, both the United States and the Soviet Union supported groups attacking allies of the other side. The United States supported dissidents attacking the pro-Soviet regime in Afghanistan and the pro-Soviet Sandinista regime in Nicaragua. The Soviet Union in turn gave assistance to leftist organizations in Western Europe and elsewhere and liberation movements that weakened US allies. Arab countries in conflict with

Israel have provided assistance to a variety of Palestinian groups as part of their efforts to weaken Israel. India and Pakistan have aided dissident groups on the other side of their common border in efforts to undermine what each sees as a potential opponent. Iran and Iraq both supported dissidents on the other side during their long war in the 1980s. In cases such as these the foreign governments frequently pursue their own agendas, which often include weakening a potential enemy, by providing support to the terrorist groups (and other insurgent groups as well) that exist in the foreign countries.

There is a significant difference between state supporters of terrorist organizations in other countries (so-called rogue states in the terminology of the twenty-first century) and permissive states. Permissive states do not interfere with the activities of terrorist groups that use their territory. They may not interfere because they lack the capacity to do so. In other cases they may fear repercussions if they attempt to crack down on the terrorist group, including attacks on their own soil or their interests abroad. States that are permissive, either through fear or lack of resources, provide less support than the rogue states that actively seek to assist foreign terrorist groups.

While some groups receive foreign support, which often makes them more effective and thus more dangerous, many of them would exist even if there were no assistance from foreign governments. Charges of foreign support, while true in some cases, do not explain the existence of dissident terrorist groups. Governments often charge that the dissident groups are receiving foreign support (even if they are not) in order to discredit their domestic opponents. If a foreign country can be blamed for the violence, then the failures of the domestic government that may actually have contributed to the outbreak of violent opposition can be explained away. Foreign governments can often become convenient scapegoats for domestic problems and for the presence of internal discontent that leads to the appearance of violent dissidents.

DIASPORA MOVEMENTS

Individuals who have migrated abroad in diaspora groups can be important supporters for terrorist organizations. **Diaspora populations** are composed of individuals from the home country who have moved abroad. These potential supporters can collectively provide important financial assistance for dissident groups in the home country. At least some of these individuals living abroad may have migrated because of their dissatisfaction with the government of their home country; thus, the diaspora can be a very logical place in which dissident groups can seek support. Members of a diaspora community can be a very willing source of support since they agree with the need for political change at home. In other cases, financial support from within the diaspora movement may involve elements of coercion from the dissident organization. Terrorist groups within a foreign country may have an existing structure within the diaspora community that will permit them to extort money from their fellow nationals. The extortion will likely be successful since a terrorist organization can be credible if threats are made against the persons living abroad or against members of their families who are still living in the home country. Since terrorist organizations have characteristics that permit them to effectively threaten to inflict harm, the collection of revolutionary taxes or donations from different groups can be easier. Of course, continuing extortion from a migrant community is likely to weaken support for the dissidents in the long run.

Diaspora communities can provide other resources to assist terrorist groups. They may contain potential recruits for later attacks. The community can also provide a safe haven for members of the group on the run; they can blend in with their fellow nationals, and they may be difficult for local police forces or security personnel to find. Of course, if the diaspora group is in a country with either a weak government or a permissive attitude towards the terrorist group, the danger of arrest would be even less. The diaspora may also be able to find ways to send arms, equipment, or other materials to the dissidents at home. Further, supporters in the diaspora can arrange to provide training for members of the groups, and in other cases they may be able to provide intelligence or scout locations for actions directed against targets associated with the home government. Migrant communities can thus effectively extend the reach of a terrorist group.

Diaspora movements have been especially important for a number of dissident groups. Irish-Americans supported efforts to create an independent Ireland when all of the island was under British rule, and they have later supported efforts to unite Northern Ireland with the Republic of Ireland. The Irish Republican Army (IRA) could depend upon Irish-Americans for financing, the purchase of weapons and other forms of support. The pressure of Irish-American voters even forced the United States to be a somewhat permissive country in terms of dealing with supporters of the IRA. Groups that raised funds for the IRA were able to do so with relatively little interference from authorities, and the IRA was never officially designated a terrorist group by the United States government. Had it been so designated, extradition of suspected terrorists, interference with fund raising, and other limitations on supporting activities would have been easier. The Palestinian diaspora has supported a variety of dissident groups in the West Bank and the Gaza Strip in their efforts to create an independent Palestinian state. The Tamil Tigers in Sri Lanka received a substantial amount of support from Tamil communities abroad which is one of the factors that permitted the group to survive for so long. Sikh militant organizations that fought to separate the Punjab from India in the 1980s also were able to depend upon significant external support from Sikh communities abroad.

FOREIGN SYMPATHIZERS

While members of migrant communities abroad can be an important source of support, there can be foreign sympathizers who are not from the home country. Like diaspora groups, they can provide finances and other support to dissident terrorist organizations. These sympathizers may share the ideology of the groups, whether it be left-wing or right-wing. In other cases they may have a religious link with the dissidents, supporting co-religionists in their efforts to practice their religion or impose their religious values in a particular state or group of states. Individuals may identify with what they see as a national liberation struggle that may be similar to their own experiences or recent history. Why the foreign sympathizers exist will be quite variable, but they can provide resources to a terrorist group.

The struggle of the Afghan resistance to the Soviet Union and the communist regime in that country clearly benefited from individual sympathizers abroad. It was not only foreign governments that provided aid but many individuals as well. Of course, many of these foreign sympathizers, including Osama bin Laden, not only provided funds but they also served as volunteer soldiers in the field in Afghanistan. Volunteers came from many parts of the world to fight against the Soviet Union and the local communist government. The experiences that these volunteers shared in Afghanistan provided the basis for cooperation and mutual support in later years. Al Qaeda has continued to benefit from private supporters. Funds have continued to flow to the organizations and its affiliated group from individuals in Saudi Arabia and elsewhere in the Islamic world. Sympathizers in a variety of countries have helped to facilitate the flow of Islamic fighters to Iraq to oppose the United States, its allies, and the new government of that country after the invasion of 2003. Individuals who sympathize with the global jihad in the United States, Western Europe, and elsewhere have undertaken independent attacks on their own in support of the objectives of Al Qaeda or have helped others to launch attacks.

Palestinians not only received support from Arab governments and the Palestinian diaspora but also from Arabs in many parts of the world who identify with the desire of the Palestinians to form their own state. Sympathetic Tamils in India provided support to Tamil rebels in Sri Lanka, and political leaders in India have had to be aware of the voting power of their own Tamil population when dealing with Sri Lanka and the former movement of Tamils for an independent or autonomous state. Rajiv Gandhi was assassinated in 1991 by a Tamil Tiger suicide bomber while he was campaigning in the Tamil area of India. The attack was in retaliation for Gandhi's policies while prime minister that had ultimately favored the government of Sri Lanka when Indian troops became involved in combat with the Tamil guerrillas. It is clear that the attackers received at least some assistance from sympathetic Tamils in India in setting up the attack. Many individuals in the newly independent African countries supported efforts of groups in the Portuguese colonies, Rhodesia, and South Africa to gain independence because of their identification with the goals of the liberation movements. The Jewish settler community in British Palestine after World War II had widespread support among the Jewish community in the United States but also in Jewish communities elsewhere in the world that identified with the settlers and the survivors of the Holocaust who had migrated to Palestine. They supplied substantial funding for the efforts to create an independent state, and these sympathetic groups were important in the efforts to smuggle arms to the Jewish paramilitaries and terrorist organizations in Palestine.

COOPERATION AMONG GROUPS

Assistance for dissident organizations can come from cooperation among groups that share similar objectives. Islamic dissident groups obviously have worked with each other based on their shared religious goals, including creating more Islamic governments in their countries and, more recently, recreating a unified Islamic community. While there have been other groups with essentially religious agendas driving their violence, few of the others have been able to develop international linkages of any consequence. Groups with objectives related to Hinduism and Sikhism have been limited to India, while groups primarily based in Christianity or other religions have been relatively few in recent years and isolated in individual countries.

Ideological groups have often formed international bonds. The radical leftist movements operating in Europe from the late 1960s to the 1980s collaborated with each other. They mounted a few joint attacks or coordinated campaigns, but probably the most important advantage cooperation provided was that, for example, a Spanish group would be able to provide logistical support and information to a German team seeking to launch an attack against a German target on Spanish soil. Leftists in different Latin American countries cooperated at times in their attacks against the conservative regimes that they opposed. Violent fascist groups occasionally supported each other before World War II. After the war right-wing groups opposed to their governments or policies have had more limited levels of cooperation. The groups that appeared in the late 1980s and later that opposed culturally different migrants to their countries in Europe have tried to work together to achieve their common objectives. There have also been indications that the extreme right in Europe and the United States have been increasingly trying to work together.

Collaboration among organizations with an ethnic base is relatively unusual unless they are dissident groups in the same empire or separatist groups in the same country. In other cases, however, such groups are geographically unique for the most part. Leftist ideological groups, however, have assisted some nationalist groups. A number of leftist organizations have regarded colonial or ethnic situations as part of a pattern of global capitalist domination and exploitation. For example, while Palestinians generally saw themselves as involved in a nationalist struggle for independence, leftists saw Israel as a capitalist outpost in the Middle East. Providing assistance to the Palestinians thus became part of the battle against the evils of global capitalism. Members of the German Red Army Faction joined with Palestinians from the **Popular Front for the Liberation of Palestine**, a leftist and nationalist group, to hijack an Air France flight in 1976. Also, in 1976 members of the **Japanese Red Army** launched an attack in Tel Aviv's Lod Airport after deplaning as a sign of solidarity with the Palestinian nationalist cause. This attack was as successful as it was because at that time Israel was not expecting such an attack from incoming Japanese passengers posing as tourists.

Cooperation among groups across national boundaries or those with similar ideologies can enhance the reach of individual groups and make them more dangerous. Cooperation among different groups is not very likely. Left-wing groups and right-wing groups are not very likely to cooperate, and they may end up battling each other in countries where both exist. Religious and nationalist groups have cooperated in Chechnya since their goals overlap. There have been some unlikely alliances. The **Revolutionary Armed Forces of Colombia (FARC)**, a leftist group opposed to the government, apparently hired experienced members of the IRA to teach members of the group how to construct bombs that would be effective in an urban setting. In Sri Lanka, the leftist **Janatha Vimukthi Peramuna** (Peoples Liberation Front) refused to cooperate with the ethnic Tamil Tigers when they both were battling against the central government. Their lack of cooperation played a role in the defeat of the JVP in 1989 and probably in the ultimate defeat of the Tamil Tigers. In Palestine, Hamas (a religiously based group) and Fatah (a nationalist secular group) have been fighting with each other rather than cooperating in their battle against Israel.

CRIMINAL ORGANIZATIONS

Another form of external support that has become more important recently has come from criminal groups. There is evidence of increasing cooperation between criminal organizations and terrorist groups operating in the same areas. Criminal groups involved in smuggling have often developed working relationships with terrorist groups since both groups have common interests in the clandestine movements of goods and people without interference by the security forces. Dissident groups and criminal organizations have some other interests that they share. Both groups are likely to be concerned about discovery by the police or security personnel. Frequently, they both want to weaken the national government – the criminal groups so that they can operate even more freely with more profit while the terrorist groups will be one step closer to forcing changes in policies or overthrowing the government. Should the dissident groups gain power, of course, this alliance of convenience with criminal elements would most likely come to an end since the two groups would now find themselves on opposite sides.

Drug trafficking has been an area of common activity for criminal and violent dissident groups. Dissident groups have even become directly involved in such trade in many parts of the world since profits from drugs can become an important source of finances for continuing the political struggle. The Taliban when it was in power in Afghanistan turned a blind eye to the export of drugs from regions under its control. The Taliban with their very fundamental religious views did not have a positive view of drug use. The drugs in question, however, were making their way to the West; thus, they were not harming Muslims for the most part. The negative impacts of the drug use were in Western societies, which were suspect in the eyes of the Taliban because the West had accepted secular ideas and had deviated so far from any religious path. In addition, the money from drug production was important for the government in its continuing efforts to gain total control of the country.

The **Shining Path** movement in Peru and the FARC in Colombia have been two leftist groups that had strong links to drug cartels since they controlled the areas that were the sources for cocaine. The Shining Path organization has been largely defeated in Peru, but FARC continues to be a major domestic political actor in Colombia. FARC has become so powerful, in fact, that there are significant areas of Colombia that are beyond effective government control. FARC continues to use guerrilla actions and terrorism to work against the government, so far with a fair amount of success. The profits from control of drug producing areas in both Peru and Colombia have been extensive enough that the guerrillas and terrorists have at times been better armed than at least the local military forces they have to deal with. Drug profits can have a corrupting effect on all groups that come into contact with it. In Colombia the pervasive effect of drug money has affected politicians and the military, paramilitary groups, and the dissidents in FARC. The dissident leadership at times seems to have been more concerned with maintaining its control over the sources of cocaine than in achieving changes in the policies of the government or attaining political power.

Some terrorist groups have become even more involved in criminal activity, focusing even more on the profits from criminal activity to fund their attempts to achieve political change. Some groups have even drifted more into criminal activity with a declining emphasis on their political goals. The IRA used a variety of criminal actions to help fund their struggle to eliminate British rule in Northern Ireland. As efforts to achieve a political solution to the violence in Northern Ireland have taken hold, some elements of the IRA have continued the criminal activities even though the political situation has changed. **The Abu Sayyaf group** in the Philippines began as an extremist Islamic group with ties to Al Qaeda. It has opposed the central Philippine government and worked for independence for the Muslim areas of the country. Abu

Sayyaf was only one of a number of groups seeking independence or autonomy for Muslim areas of the Philippines. It was unique in that its leaders and the initial core of its membership came from veterans of the war in Afghanistan against the Soviet Union and the local communist regime. When the organization was first formed, it initially had direct connections with Al Qaeda. The group engaged in some spectacular kidnappings of foreign tourists in Malaysia and the Philippines. The ransoms from these kidnappings helped provide funding for other group activities. The group suffered important losses in confrontations with government security forces, including the death of some of the original leaders. With a change in leadership the group has appeared to be much more concerned with the financial benefits from criminal activity and has been less active in the political arena. The group splintered with some components being almost solely engaged in criminal activities while other parts still undertook violent actions with political objectives.

CHANGING PATTERNS OF EXTERNAL SUPPORT

In the days of the Cold War, external support from foreign states was quite frequent. Each side supported opposition groups on the other side, even if they had no ideological affinity with the groups involved. The end of the Cold War did not end foreign support entirely, but it did reduce it. It has become much more difficult for a country to support violent dissidents in the United States or one of its allies, even in an indirect fashion, given the possible negative repercussions from US action and the absence of a strong superpower protector. There are still pairs of states engaged in disputes or with high levels of tension, such as India and Pakistan, where the temptation to support groups on the other side of the border will be very great indeed. Most governments will be quick to take advantage of opportunities to weaken a potential opponent that domestic terrorist groups in other countries provide.

Diaspora movements have become more important in recent years, perhaps because it is easier to collect and transfer money around the globe and to mobilize other resources than in the past. In today's world the virtually instantaneous electronic transfers of funds can be made to virtually any place in the world, and air travel permits the movement of key personnel with great rapidity as well. Money can also be transferred from country to country by a variety of informal mechanisms that are difficult to regulate or trade. If a terrorist organization can mobilize support from migrants, it can be very difficult for governments to interrupt the flow of funds, especially when the money is moving through the informal channels. The same can hold true for foreign supporters and sympathizers in general. While large contributions may be very useful for the dissidents, small contributions from multiple sources will be extremely difficult to track or predict effectively. Cooperation between terrorist groups and criminal organizations is now another important concern for many governments, and criminal groups can provide significant resources for terrorists. When drug trafficking is involved, as is often the case, the increase in resources can be quite substantial.

CONCLUSIONS

Terrorist groups must find a base of domestic support in order to have any hope of bringing about changes in policies or governments. While all governments have unhappy citizens, unhappy citizens will not necessarily support terrorist organizations. If the dissidents can successfully follow a strategy of provoking a government into overreacting to the threat, they may be able to increase their support while neutralizing some other sources of support for the government. Whereas all terrorist groups, except those that are a foreign power or intelligence agency, must have domestic support, groups can attract foreign support. This external support can be from a foreign government or governments, from diasporas, from other foreign sympathizers, from like-minded terrorist organizations in other countries, or from criminal networks. Of course, in most cases it is probably groups that have already demonstrated their ability to challenge their government that are best able to attract some form of external support rather than external support making a very weak domestic organization a major threat. This foreign support of all kinds will often increase the effectiveness of the dissidents, and it can make their activities more effective, and even more deadly.

KEY TERMS

Abu Sayyaf, diaspora population, Janatha Vimokthi Peramuna, Popular Front for the Liberation of Palestine, Red Army Faction, Revolutionary Armed Forces of Colombia (FARC), Shining Path

FURTHER READING

Fair, C. C. (2005) "Diaspora Involvement in Insurgencies: Insights from the Khalistan and Tamil Eelam Movements," *Nationalism and Ethnic Politics*, 11, 1: 125–56.

This article provides a valuable overview on the importance of diaspora communities for dissident groups involved in struggles in the home country.

Rodell, P. A. (2007) "Separatist Insurgency in the Southern Philippines," in A. T. H. Tan (ed.), *A Handbook of Terrorism and Insurgency in Southeast Asia*. Cheltenham: Edward Elgar, 225–47.

This chapter discusses the Abu Sayyaf group and other militant separatist groups in the Muslim areas of the Philippines, including their tactics and somewhat varied goals and their foreign connections.

Stern, J. (2000) "Pakistan's Jihad Culture," *Foreign Affairs*, 79, 6: 115–26.

Stern provides insights on how local conditions can lead to support for terrorists in neighboring territories. In the case of Pakistan the toleration of the government and local support for terrorist activities are both important.

Williams, P. (2008) "Terrorist Financing and Organized Crime: Nexus, Appropriation, or Transformation?" in T. J. Biersteker and S. E. Eckert (eds.), *Countering the Financing of Terrorism*, London: Routledge, 126–49.

This chapter provides a very good overview of some of the connections between terrorist groups and criminal organizations.

WHAT CAN BE DONE TO COUNTER TERRORISM?

Governments around the world have tried a variety of approaches in dealing with terrorism. Sederberg (2003) has suggested that terrorism can be dealt with as the equivalent of war, as criminal activity, and as a disease. Some of these efforts are consistent with views that regard terrorism as warfare as was apparent with the announcement of the Global War on Terrorism by President George Bush, Jr. The invasion of Afghanistan in the aftermath of the attacks on September 11, 2001 is another example of a war approach. Russia has adopted a similar strategy for dealing with the unrest and terrorist attacks originating in Chechnya relying in large measure on military actions to deal with the unrest. A second approach focuses on dealing with terrorism primarily through the police and court systems. Any meaningful act of terrorism is going to violate existing national laws in any country; thus, it can always be considered criminal activity and dealt with accordingly. Most terrorist groups are short-lived precisely because their initial attacks expose them to reactions by the police and security forces, and they are quickly discovered and prosecuted or eliminated in other ways. Other responses by governments involve considering terrorism a disease where the causes as well as the symptoms must be dealt with. In this view the appropriate response for countries attempting to get to the root causes that underlie the rise of the terrorist groups. Although there is no one root cause of terrorism, in specific cases governments may realize that neglect of a particular region or discrimination against a portion of the population may have created fertile ground for the appearance and spread of terrorism. As a consequence, a government may attempt to change policies. Of course, when governments are actually supporting domestic factions that use terror against a group of its own citizens, the government will obviously choose to do nothing to deal with the violence. When governments are facing violence by dissidents, however, they will often take counterterrorism actions in keeping with one or the other of these perspectives.

REPRESSION

Virtually the first response of any government facing a terrorist threat will be efforts to capture and eliminate the terrorist group. While the police activities may be seen as routine by the government and many citizens, they are likely to be seen as repression by any dissidents who have decided to resort to violence, as well as by their sympathizers and supporters. As noted above, police and security forces frequently can deal with these violent political opponents reasonably quickly, explaining why most groups last for only a relatively short time. Terrorist groups are likely to be particularly vulnerable when they first appear because the members are learning their craft, and they cannot develop the practical experience that can only come with time.

Even though many violent dissidents are quickly dealt with, there are some groups that have been able to survive the initial stage of scrutiny by the police or security forces. There are times when the authorities fail to appreciate the severity of the threat and thus give the dissidents a chance to grow to the point where they constitute a more serious threat. If the government has been neglecting a region of the country for a lengthy period of time, it could easily miss the development of increased unrest and the creation of potentially violent groups. In other cases, a terrorist group may survive the early stages of a campaign by sheer luck – and some groups that actually prepare very well for a campaign of violent activity can be undone by accident. Some groups have come to the attention of authorities when there is an accident in a house or apartment where they are making bombs. External support may enable a group to deal with the initial attempts at repression or the organization may be able to take advantage of a weak domestic government or a weak government in a neighboring state to create a relatively safe base of operations.

Once a group gets past the initial stages and grows to be more powerful, for whatever reason, the government will have to rely on more extensive efforts to eliminate the threat. More resources will be devoted to police and security forces. Rewards may be offered for citizen assistance, and new restrictive laws may be put into place. In more authoritarian states suspects can be arrested and brought in for questioning, and they can even be tortured. Indefinite detention may occur for dissidents and for any one suspected of supporting the terrorists. Family members can even be threatened if the terrorists are operating from safe bases in a foreign state or in an area uncontrolled by a weak government. Governments may also begin to give support to citizens' groups that attack those suspected of supporting the terrorists. They can also unleash death squads and engage in extrajudicial executions in an attempt to eliminate support for the terrorists.

Greater repression will often work against terrorist groups. Since terrorism is a weapon of the weak, the dissidents will frequently be overmatched. The governments of Argentina in the 1970s dealt with terrorism from the left by simply having unofficial death squads kidnap suspects who were then interrogated and tortured, and then executed. The government of the Islamic Republic of Iran in its early days was able to defeat campaigns by secular and leftist groups with the liberal use of repressive measures. The government in Russia has been able so far to at least contain the unrest in Chechnya through repression and more general (and sometimes indiscriminate) attacks on regions which have supported the Chechen dissidents.

PHYSICAL SECURITY

Increased security is one inevitable response to terrorism. Metal detectors in airports and elsewhere, barriers to prevent direct access for vehicles (loaded with explosives or not), fences, and other similar defenses against attacks all can provide some protection. Of course, it is impossible to provide perfect security for every facility or individual. All government officials cannot be protected all the time. Similarly, every building, monument, power line, or public gathering can not be made totally secure. Israel with some of the best security measures and well-developed sources of intelligence gathering in the world has not been able to prevent suicide attacks and other conventional attacks on its soil. Terrorists have an advantage in that they can always find vulnerable targets. They do not have to attack the facilities that are well guarded. While perfect security is not possible, security improvements for key areas are undoubtedly wise. Nuclear power facilities have the capacity to be used to cause major damage if an "accident" can be staged. Dangerous biological strains or chemical weapons need to be carefully guarded. Even though the dangers of terrorists accessing such materials may be slim, the potential damage that can result warrants enhanced security.

Although enhanced security appears to be a worthwhile objective, it does have its negative side. The costs of providing security can be high for both the government and the private sector. Ultimately, the money devoted to greater security is not as productive as other economic uses since it does not add to the stock of products in a national economy, even though at least some security is necessary to avoid great losses. Greater security will also have indirect costs in the form of lost opportunities. Each pound, euro, or dollar spent on security by a government is a pound, euro, or dollar that is not available for education, research, medical care, housing, or other programs. For private companies it is less money for research and development, higher wages, or investment in equipment or new plants. Once terrorists have been able to force changes in security measures with the accompanying costs, they have already attained some level of success. Governments and private companies will have to balance the costs of security with a reasonable assessment of the severity of the threats.

INTELLIGENCE GATHERING

Collecting intelligence on organizations that are attacking the state or its citizens is inevitably an important counterterrorism technique. If information on the members or their plans can be uncovered, it will be much easier to deal with them, either by repression or by other means. When government agents or informers have been able to penetrate the dissident organization, counterterrorism successes, of course, are much more likely. The fear of informers can force the dissidents to invest scarce resources in protecting themselves from discovery by the security forces. It could even be productive for the security agencies to suggest that a thwarted attack was due to inside information, *even if it was not*, as part of an attempt to sow dissension in the ranks of the terrorist organization.

Security agencies also rely on information gathered from the public. Individuals may voluntarily provide such information – out of a sense of civic duty, for financial reward, a greater fear of security personnel than of retribution by the dissidents, or for personal reasons. Information may also be extracted from suspects under arrest by using torture or threats to family members, although such information is often of limited value since it may not be accurate because individuals under torture may try to tell the interrogators what they want to hear. In today's modern societies, computers can be programmed to highlight suspicious patterns from internet use, mobile phones, or emails. Once individuals have been identified with these processes, they can be more carefully scrutinized and subject to greater surveillance. If attacks do occur, forensic evidence can provide leads to the attackers. When investigators were able to identify the vehicle used in the 1993 attack on the World Trade Center in New York City, they were then able to track down the persons responsible.

Gathering intelligence is likely to be easier for a larger group of dissidents since there will be more methods that can be used, including greater opportunities to infiltrate a government agent or to find an informant. In a larger organization, however, it is likely to be more difficult to disrupt with any single intelligence gathering operation or activity by police or security forces. Smaller groups may be easier to disrupt since they do not have as many personnel and have fewer resources, although they may be harder to penetrate since members will be well known to each other and intelligence gathering much more difficult. Leaderless resistance styles of operation have made intelligence gathering much more difficult since only the members of each small cell actually know what they are planning. They also cannot provide information on large numbers of other dissidents. Even an agent or informer with access to the leaders of a loosely connected network will be unable to learn any details on many planned attacks.

ATTACKING FINANCIAL SOURCES

Counterterrorist agencies have gone after the financial assets of terrorist groups. When such assets have been found, they can be frozen by governments, making it more difficult for the group to buy arms or explosives or to support the activists undertaking the violent operations. Efforts to intercept the flow of finances to dissidents are frequently easy for governments to utilize since many countries already have mechanisms in place to attempt to track the financial flows of criminal organizations. Because existing techniques and personnel were available for use against criminal groups, they could be quickly adapted and used as part of a counterterrorist program. Existing intelligence efforts can also increase the effectiveness of these efforts.

There have been some successes in seizing money and assets or stopping the flow of funds to the dissidents, but there have been problems as well. Efforts to stop the flow of funds to Al Qaeda via Islamic charities, for example, have stopped not only funds for terrorists but donations to real charities. As a consequence, charitable funds will not be available to help those in need. It is possible that the absence of funds from the charities might increase discontent in some countries and even lead to a greater likelihood of terrorist outbreaks in some cases. Although the interdiction of finances can be successful at times, it cannot be a solution to the problem of terrorism since terrorism is usually a low cost style of warfare; terrorists will still manage to launch attacks with minimal resources. Terrorist groups have also been innovative in terms of finding alternative means of financing their activities, including converting funds to gold or diamonds, engaging in petty crime, using profits from legitimate business investments, and relying on informal mechanisms of transferring funds that can avoid interdiction.

RETALIATION

Governments may try to retaliate against terrorist groups. Any retaliation must depend upon the existence of valuable intelligence information if it is going to be effective. Of course, under normal circumstances if retaliation is possible, the authorities may already have enough information to arrest the members of a group –

although in a democracy they may not have enough information for a conviction in a court of law. The retaliation could either be through military action or with covert operations. Retaliation may be more effective when there are identifiable foreign supporters for the groups. The toppling of the Taliban regime in Afghanistan removed an important supporter of Al Qaeda. Other countries have stopped supporting groups on foreign soil when faced with economic or other sanctions as well as international diplomatic pressure. At other times, retaliation is not very effective. Israel has launched numerous attacks against the countries that have supported Palestinian groups in the past without any consistent reduction in support in many cases. Even when foreign countries did reduce support, the Palestinians continued their efforts. Strikes against Palestinian camps and training facilities in neighboring countries have hurt these nationalists at times but have hardly destroyed either the broad Palestinian movement or specific organizations. Israel also retaliated against the PLO and Palestinian Authority after the **Oslo Accords** had created that body, often without any major declines in the level of terrorist attacks. In fact, at times retaliation has led to an increase in the scale of terrorist attacks.

Related to the concept of retaliation has been the idea of "targeted killings," which is a euphemism for assassination. Such killings are intended to eliminate leaders or to punish individuals for participation in previous attacks – and to send a warning to others. Killing individuals may hurt organizations, but it is always possible that the dead leaders will be replaced by someone even more dangerous. Other individuals who are killed may become very important symbolic martyrs for the cause. Israel has engaged in a policy of targeted killings for years. A special squad tracked down and killed many of the individuals linked to the 1972 Munich Olympic attacks. Although a number of individuals were killed in retaliation, it had no obvious effect on the level of continued Palestinian attacks in the 1970s and 1980s. Moreover, Israel with obviously good intelligence sources has been able to kill many of the leaders of Hamas, yet the organization has persisted and continues to oppose Israel and its policies. The attacks against Hamas may even have given the group an electoral advantage in elections for the Palestinian Authority since Israel obviously considered the group to be the greatest threat; thus, a vote for Hamas could be seen as a vote against Israel and its policies.

Successful terrorist actions can lead to increased attention by the police or security forces, which can qualify as a form of retaliation because the dissidents have become important enough or dangerous enough for the government to track down its members. With the increased attention, many groups can be defeated. In one sense they will have become the victims of their own successes. The **Symbionese Liberation Army** in California in the 1970s had much greater freedom to operate until they kidnapped Patty Hearst. This spectacular action brought so much attention that it was eliminated as a threat relatively quickly. The attention that came with the kidnapping led the police to expend much greater efforts on finding and defeating the group. Aum Shinrikyo in Japan avoided excessive attention until it launched the attack on subway passengers in 1995. As a result of that attack there was a major government investigation, and the group was quickly eliminated as a terrorist threat.

SPECIAL FORCES

Many countries have special counterterrorism units, which are brought into play to deal with situations involving terrorists. They have specially trained police or military forces designed to deal with situations in which terrorism groups have captured buildings or airliners and/or have taken hostages. In the United Kingdom, the Special Air Services Regiment has been the key anti-terrorist unit. In Germany it is a special unit within the border police. In other countries it is often elite formations such as commandos, rangers, or marines that are given the task of dealing with terrorists. In the United States it is either special units of the Federal Bureau of Investigation or local police forces that deal with these situations. There is little doubt that such units can be important, especially for dealing with building takeovers and hostage situations. There have been both successes and failures with such units. Leftists seized the Japanese embassy in Lima, Peru in December 1996, and Peruvian commandos then spent months preparing an assault that would rescue all but one of the remaining hostages. When Russian special forces sought to rescue hostages from a Moscow theatre in 2002, more than 100 of the over 800 civilians died as a special gas was used to immobilize the Chechen nationalists in control of the building. Israeli special forces have had a number of successful rescue operations, but there has also been failures. Even the failures suggest, however, that the absence of such units could lead to even greater losses of life among hostages or leave a government no choice but to negotiate with groups holding the hostages.

The creation, existence, and training of these special units constitutes an admission by governments that terrorist groups will at least occasionally be successful in gaining control of buildings, transportation vehicles, or people and that a specialized, active response is necessary. Since most major countries have such groups, it is a tacit admission that not all of these types of operations by dissidents can be prevented and that total security is impossible.

INTERNATIONAL COOPERATION

Another mechanism for dealing with terrorist groups is international cooperation. Diplomatic efforts can provide a means to weaken or to deal with violent groups. Cooperation among intelligence agencies often occurs either by prior arrangement or in an ad hoc fashion, and such cooperation can be useful, although it is more difficult when countries have had antagonistic relationships in the past (or continue to have them in the present). Since no intelligence agency can have people on the ground in every country, local personnel are likely to be more effective for gathering information on their own soil.

Diplomatic efforts have been made to reach global accords on definitions of terrorism or for the banning of terrorist organizations. These attempts have not yet been particularly successful since there will always be governments that fear such agreements could be used against groups that they favor or foreign dissident organizations that are popular in their countries. In most cases no Arab government wants to deal with the popular discontent that would occur if it extradited a Palestinian accused of terrorism to Israel for trial. It could increase popular discontent if the suspects were extradited to the United States, a European nation, or even other Arab countries. Although there has been no global agreement on a definition of terrorism or terrorist groups, there have been some accomplishments. International protocols exist criminalizing certain actions such as skyjacking, piracy, and other activities. While less than comprehensive, they do provide a mechanism for dealing with at least some of the methods available to violent groups.

In addition to such global arrangements, regional and bilateral agreements can lay the groundwork for successful counterterrorism strategies. The European Union has been relatively successful in reaching such agreements and has facilitated a variety of cooperative counterterrorism efforts among the members. The governments with more established intelligence agencies have been able to provide assistance to countries with weaker security forces. Various European countries have cooperated with the United States as well. In other situations bilateral collaboration is possible. The British and French intelligence agencies have working relationships with many former parts of their empires. Russian security (and military) forces have been present in many of the countries that used to be part of the old Soviet Union. The United States has treaty arrangements with several countries such as Canada, Australia, and Japan that facilitate cooperation in dealing with terrorist groups.

Diplomacy has a role to play in counterterrorism efforts. It can facilitate intelligence gathering and the disruption of financial flows to terrorist organizations. International arrangements might also be able to limit – but probably not eliminate – the assistance that can come from immigrant populations or foreign sympathizers. International cooperation might also provide opportunities in at least some cases for more successful retaliation and repression of groups. Ultimately, diplomatic efforts will not provide a solution by themselves, but they can weaken terrorist groups and can even provide some assistance in dealing with the underlying causes of terrorism.

CONCESSIONS AND REFORMS

Even though governments may be reluctant to admit it, changes in policies may be a worthwhile means of undermining support for terrorist groups. Dissident organizations often draw upon genuine sources of discontent that exist within a society. A region or particular ethnic or religious group may be suffering from neglect or even active discrimination. A social or economic group may be in a similar situation. The government can undertake reforms to address these underlying problems that have generated discontent, thus making it more difficult for a terrorist group to attract material and financial support and recruits from a region or population group. Changes in policies could be effective in limiting external support as well. Such reforms could include government investment in the development of infrastructure or the provision of education or health care. This type of effort may require foreign assistance if the domestic government has been unable to provide such opportunities in the past because of an ongoing lack of economic resources. Terrorist groups may rely on a spoiling strategy and launch attacks to undermine the reforms since they recognize the danger to their objectives that could come with such efforts by the government. Government officials, workers, and teachers could become targets, and they might be especially vulnerable to such spoiling attacks.

Most governments will prefer to launch reform programs rather than make direct concessions to a terrorist group. Reforms can be presented as normal policy decisions that result from an initiative from the political leadership while concessions are seen as a response, even a coerced response, to very direct demands from dissident groups. If the dissidents are demanding regional autonomy or a national liberation front is seeking independence, then the granting of autonomy or independence is obviously a concession. If dissident groups are demanding free election in a non-democratic society, the holding of such elections would also clearly constitute a concession by the existing rulers. Dissident groups may also use terrorist actions against foreign targets as noted in Chapter 5 in an effort to gain concessions. They may be attempting to coerce the foreign governments to change their policies of support. They might also want a foreign government to pressure their domestic government to undertake specific reforms or to grant particular concessions. Attracting international publicity for their problems could also have similar effects in terms of leading to changes in policies by either the domestic government or foreign supporters of the domestic leadership.

Even though reforms or concessions are one possible solution to terrorist violence, and one that may attempt to get at the root causes of the violence, they are not always possible. Governments may face pressures to adopt changes that reflect the views of a minority that are not acceptable to the rest of the population. Religious extremists – whether Christian, Jewish, Muslim, Buddhist, or Hindu – may be demanding the incorporation of religious values into law that are opposed by substantial majorities. Dissident organizations with particular ideological demands may want the effective disenfranchisement of their opponents. Violent groups with racist views may be attempting to drive minorities or particular categories of immigrants out of the country and to prevent the entry of minorities. In situations such as these and others like them, concessions may not be possible and clearly in many cases will not be desirable.

In other situations, a government may face violence from extremist groups with mutually exclusive objectives. In 1962 the French government had reached the point where it was willing to concede independence to Algeria after a protracted guerrilla and terrorist campaign by the Algerian National Liberation Front. It then had to deal with a terrorist campaign by an unhappy settler community in Algeria and their supporters in France. Any concession to one group was a clear provocation to the other. In the 1970s, Turkey faced serious outbreaks of violence from both the left and the right. There was no set of policy concessions and reform that would have appeased both sides. The Turkish military eventually intervened in the face of the continuing and escalating violence. The military government cracked down on both the left and the right, but its policies were more in the direction of changes desired by the right and against the interests of the leftist dissidents. In Iraq in the years after the invasion in 2003, it is difficult to conceive of any changes in policies that the newly created government or the United States could have made that would have been effective in meeting the demands of Iraqi nationalists, Sunni Arab opponents, various groups of Shia Arab dissidents, and the global jihadist movement supported by Al Qaeda and affiliated organizations that were active in the country. These groups have obviously mutually antagonistic objectives. In a broader arena, the reality of world politics makes it unlikely that the United States will be able to withdraw completely from the Middle East or that Russia will be able to ignore problems in neighboring countries in Central Asia as demanded by some groups. Further, it is not possible for the West to stop the processes that come with globalization that have disrupted local societies and economies even if it wanted to.

In the final analysis, concessions and reforms cannot be a solution to all terrorist situations. If an elite cannot hope to remain in power if there are free elections and they believe that repression is likely to work, then reforms are not going to be attempted. Even when a government is willing to attempt concession, competing groups can have mutually contradictory demands. Moreover, governments may lack the resources to implement the necessary reforms. Finally, the demands of the dissidents may prove to be unacceptable to the political leaders, to domestic society, or to important groups of the domestic population.

NEGOTIATIONS

Almost all governments proclaim that they will never negotiate with terrorists. Others suggest that negotiating with terrorists, just as granting concessions to terrorists, only encourages the terrorists by granting them a status equal to the government or that by giving in to demands leads to even more demands. Negotiations also imply that the government is willing to make at least some concessions to the dissidents in return for an end to the violence. Practically speaking, however, governments and the private sector almost always engage in explicit or implicit negotiations with terrorists. When groups seize airliners complete with passengers and demand that a list of grievances be read over the air or published in a newspaper in exchange for the release of some of the hostages, most governments will agree to the demands. In these circumstances, there actually are limited options available to the government. The dissidents have already achieved publicity with the hostage taking; if the government refuses these simple demands, the dissidents may gain even more publicity and the government may share part of the blame for any loss of life. When terrorists demand safe passage out of the country in return for the release of remaining hostages, governments frequently agree, especially if the country where the terrorists are headed has made it known that the terrorists will face penalties if they fail to live up to their part of the bargain.

A more complicated situation occurs when terrorists seize hostages or undertake bombing campaigns demanding that "imprisoned comrades" be released. Governments do not want convicted terrorists set free to continue their activities, and such releases are moral victories for the dissidents. There is little doubt that successful releases will lead to similar demands in the future. As a consequence, governments will try to avoid negotiating in these situations. There are times, however, when it is difficult to avoid some negotiations. If a planeload of hostages from many different countries is being held, a government may wish to avoid the negative international publicity from the deaths of hostages because of its refusal to even discuss issues with terrorists. In this situation negotiations and concessions may be especially expedient if a relatively unknown group is making the demands. A well known group has to be aware of the possibilities of negative publicity for its causes, and a threat to kill hostages may actually be a bluff. A new group, even if it is an offshoot of an existing group or a false front, would be more likely to carry out its threats. Even though government security experts may know that the groups are linked, they will still have to deal with adverse domestic and international public opinion that would be present with the death of hostages.

Although governments may be forced to negotiate with terrorists in some circumstances, they may be reluctant to engage in more direct negotiations in an effort to resolve conflicts. Reluctant as governments may be, such negotiations do occur. The Oslo Accords that Israel and the PLO agreed to, began as negotiations between private individuals. The leaders of the PLO and the Israeli political leaders were aware of these talks, and their initial successes then proceeded to more formal talks that led to a signed agreement. The Oslo Accords led to the creation of the Palestinian Authority and an element of self-government for the Palestinians. The PLO also agreed to recognize Israel and to renounce the use of terrorism. The conflicts between various anti-colonial movements and the colonial powers were inevitably resolved through talks between the two sides. Direct negotiations do not always work, of course, but they have the possibility of ending a conflict. Indirect

> The Japanese Red Army, a leftist group, seized Japanese embassies and other targets abroad taking hostages. It then gained concessions from the Japanese government in the 1970s and 1980s. The willingness of the Japanese government to pay ransoms or make other concessions contributed to terrorism becoming a global problem. (Wilkinson 2003: 124)

or direct negotiations, even when they fail may be an effective counterterrorism technique in other ways. The negotiating process may give the government leaders and their security forces greater insights into the nature of their opponents, their goals, and their possible weaknesses. The talks may also provide opportunities for gathering useful intelligence that could be helpful in defeating the dissidents when the talks break down.

DEMOBILIZING GROUP MEMBERS

If counterterrorism programs are successful, it may be necessary to reintegrate surviving members of the group back into society. For small groups, most of the members will be dead or in prison. For larger groups there may be more difficulties in returning members to a more normal life, especially if the struggle has been a long one. Veterans of guerrilla struggles and terrorist campaigns will lack some of the skills necessary for civilian employment or the necessary job experiences. Local businesses may be reluctant to hire them. There are no easy answers to the reintegration of individuals into their domestic societies. It is difficult to evaluate the success of programs designed to reintegrate members back into civilian society. Some of the group members will remain wedded to the process of struggle and the need to defeat the enemy. They will not be satisfied with the gains made by the dissident groups since there are few groups, if any, that will achieve all their goals. As a consequence, these committed dissidents frequently form splinter groups that seek to continue their struggles to achieve even more of the original goals. The true hardliners are unwilling to give up. They will not accept autonomy instead of independence. Ireland

> As far as negotiating with terrorists "it is not at all clear that refusing 'to talk to terrorists' shortens their campaigns any more than entering into negotiations prolongs them." (Cronin 2009: 35)

faced a civil war after the creation of the Irish Free State in 1922 instigated by hardliners who were dissatisfied with the treaty with Great Britain. Of course, other hardliners intermittently kept up the battle to incorporate Northern Ireland into the Irish Free State. When the PLO agreed to the Oslo Accords, a number of groups left the PLO and created the rejectionist front against the agreements. They were unwilling to accept the more limited concessions by Israel that were part of the accords. Thus, even success can generate new terrorist problems for governments.

COUNTERTERRORISM AND CIVIL LIBERTIES

While there are a variety of counterterrorism strategies that governments can pursue, at the same time there are issues involving the civil liberties of residents and citizens. When security is increased in the face of terrorist attacks, governments and their citizens have to consider how much freedom they are willing to trade in order to have greater security. This issue is particularly important for democratic states since a respect for civil liberties is what helps to define a democratic society. Civil liberties issues can also be important for authoritarian systems since many of them generally do follow a rule of law where individuals are only arrested if they violate existing laws, however restrictive those laws might be. While there may be only a few freedoms present in authoritarian societies, limitations on these few freedoms can run the risk of driving more people into the ranks of the dissidents.

The attacks on 9/11 led to an increased concern about security in many parts of the world. In the United States, it became easier for authorities to obtain search warrants and to conduct covert electronic surveillance and wiretaps. Since secrecy was important in these situations, individuals would not even know they had been subjected to searches or that their bank accounts and other records has been accessed and scrutinized. A no-fly list was instituted which prohibited persons from boarding aircraft because of their suspected connections to terrorist groups. Presumption of guilt rather than a presumption of innocence is present with such a non-fly list. Guantanamo Bay became a detention area for individuals seized abroad for involvement in terrorist actions. The naval base became a prison camp for enemy combatants who could be kept there indefinitely with little or no prospect of ever being brought to trial. While many of the individuals were eventually released to their home countries, some have remained. US government agencies also began practicing more intensive interrogation techniques that bordered on torture and in at least some cases constituted torture. Since more extreme forms of torture were not permitted under US laws and standard practices, the policy of **rendition** was created. With rendition suspects were transported to countries friendly to the United States where they would be tortured by local security personnel. Any intelligence that was gathered as a result of the torture was then passed on to the United States. The US agencies managed to remain within the technical letter of the law by not practicing torture themselves, but they clearly contributed to the practice elsewhere. As unacceptable as all these practices are, the situation was made worse because there were at least some cases where innocent people suffered as a consequence.

In the United States one practice that cannot be routinely used is data mining. This technique involves sophisticated computer searches of all types of government records and files, computer activity, bank transactions, and all kinds of information. The computer searches are routinely applied to all citizens and residents. The data mining can be used to identify individuals with suspicious profiles who will be subjected to greater scrutiny. In the United States, the generalized fear of an overbearing government has meant that government agencies cannot share information with each other. The CIA, FBI, and Homeland Security cannot access records of other agencies except with search warrants that specify a single individual and provide probable cause to justify the search. In Western Europe, citizens have been more accepting of information sharing and data mining does occur and has identified as least some individuals engaged in suspicious activities.

Questions about civil liberties have appeared before 9/11. Israel has faced the issue with its policies in the West Bank and Gaza Strip since the 1980s. There have been long-term detentions without any trials, at least the occasional use of torture, widespread curfews that make the conducting of business and maintaining crops and herds very difficult, destruction of homes as a form of reprisal for opposition, and other practices. While Israeli authorities have greater freedom in the occupied territories than on their own soil, the Israeli Supreme Court has ruled against some of the actions that have been undertaken in the name of security.

The United Kingdom resorted to practices in Northern Ireland that removed protections normally in place for citizens. New laws beginning in the 1970s gave the government longer periods of time to hold persons on suspicion of terrorism before they had to appear before a judge. There was more freedom to interrogate the persons being held. These practices only applied to terrorism suspects and not to persons accused of ordinary crime. Suspected IRA members were detained indefinitely without trial (preventative detention). When there were trials, the trials did not have juries, leaving it to the judge to determine guilt or innocence. The government had to resort to this type of trial since members of juries were being intimidated by the IRA. If the juries provided guilty verdicts, members of the juries or their family members were subject to reprisals. As a consequence, the established methods of jury trials no longer worked.

One consequence of special government laws and special processes designed to heighten security has been the creation of **suspect communities**. Irish Catholics became such a suspect community in the United Kingdom where presumption of guilt was frequent. Palestinians and Arab citizens of Israel were also suspect communities. In the aftermath of 9/11, the Madrid train bombings, and the London transport attacks, Muslims have become suspect in many countries. Even though members of the groups in question may be more likely to join or support terrorist organizations, many members of the groups will not. Such suspicions not only create problems for the individuals with the authorities, but they are likely to limit employment or other opportunities. It also becomes more difficult to integrate these individuals into the broader national community. One consequence of this trend may then be that the alienated individuals are more open to recruitment by radical, and even violent, dissident groups.

Infringements on existing civil liberties, whether they are the extensive freedoms in a democracy or the more limited ones in an authoritarian society, can play into the hands of dissident groups that follow a provocation strategy. The limitations that are imposed, if they do not work, might drive more people towards supporting the dissidents out of anger with the government. Portions of the populations that are less sympathetic to the dissidents could move into a position of neutrality instead of support for the government as a consequence of the increased restrictions. While restrictions on civil liberties might make it easier to deal with terrorists, they could also be counterproductive by alienating individuals or groups. Maintaining existing levels, on the other hand, could mean that it might take longer to meet the immediate threat from terrorists but that the public will continue to support the current system and that future threats are minimized.

CONCLUSIONS

Whether terrorism is viewed in the context of war, crime, or disease will affect which methods of counterterrorism that are chosen. Repression is always going to be used, but will be most often relied upon within the context of viewing terrorism as crime. Retaliation is likely within the context of a war on terrorism. International cooperation may be useful in all contexts. Concessions, reforms, and negotiations would be most often relied upon if terrorism is considered from the point of view of treating a disease. The view taken by the counterterrorism agencies and governments will influence the particular mix of strategies for dealing with violent dissidents that they choose.

There are many counterterrorism techniques that are available to governments. No one technique is a "magic bullet" that will always work to deal with every terrorist situation. There is a tendency for proponents of one approach to argue that this approach is the solution to terrorism in all or almost all circumstances. In fact, any proposal of one solution to terrorism is guaranteed to be wrong at

It is even possible that increased security and additional limitations on civil liberties will not only weaken democracy but that such actions would lead to an increase of internal discontent that will actually increase the likelihood of terrorism in the future. (Sederberg 2003: 273)

least some of the time. Terrorism is a technique that is used by an immense variety of groups arising from many different situations and from many different causes involving groups seeking different objectives. As a consequence, counterterrorist strategies must be tailored to individual circumstances, which, of course, is much more difficult for governments and security forces than simply following a standard blueprint. What works in one situation will fail in others. Governments in many cases will also have to be careful of the effects of policies or a mix of policies on existing civil liberties. Of the various techniques mentioned above, intelligence gathering will always be extremely valuable. Greater security will be valuable in protecting targets, such as biological laboratories or nuclear power plants, that would be extremely dangerous if they fell into terrorist hands. The value and emphasis of other techniques will vary according to circumstances.

KEY TERMS

Guantanamo Bay, Japanese Red Army, leaderless resistance, Oslo Accords, rendition, suspect communities, Symbionese Liberation Army

FURTHER READING

Banks, W. C., R. de Nevers, and M. B. Wallerstein (2008) *Combating Terrorism: Strategies and Approaches*, Washington DC: CQ Press.

This volume is one among many books on strategies of counterterrorism, and one that places the efforts within broader perspectives.

Heymann, P. B. (2003) *Terrorism, Freedom, and Security*. Cambridge, MA: MIT Press.

Heymann discusses various measures that can be taken in reaction to terrorist activities, including the potential tensions between freedom and security.

Horgan, J. and K. Braddock (2010) "Rehabilitating the Terrorists? Challenges in Assessing the Effectiveness of De-Radicalization Programs," *Terrorism and Political Violence*, 22, 2: 267–91.

This article is one of the few works that considers the problems of reintegrating former militants into society. It includes a discussion and evaluation of five programs from Indonesia, Northern Ireland, Colombia, Saudi Arabia, and Yemen.

Sederberg, P. C. (2003) "Global Terrorism: Problems of Challenge and Response," in C. W. Kegley, Jr. (ed.), *The New Global Terrorism: Characteristics, Causes, Controls*. Upper Saddle River, NJ: Prentice Hall, 267–84.

Sederberg provides a very useful characterization of the types of responses that governments can take to deal with terrorism and some of the consequences of these characterizations.

8

WHAT ARE SOME OF
THE MAJOR GROUPS?

The previous chapters have discussed terrorism from a number of perspectives. At various times some well-known examples of terrorist groups or situations have been used to elaborate upon key points, but no group has been discussed in any detail. The material below will consequently discuss some specific groups in terms of the various ideas and concepts already discussed. The groups included are the Assassins, Al Qaeda, the Irish Republican Army, Hizballah, the Ku Klux Klan, ETA, the Tamil Tigers, the **Naxalites** in India, and government supported terrorism in Zimbabwe. These are some of the better known examples and in the case of the dissident groups, ones that have survived for longer periods of time than others. Although books have been written about them, the discussions to follow will be much briefer. First, however, it is important to clarify that terrorism has been a technique for centuries and is not just a recent phenomenon.

TERRORISM IS NOT NEW

It is often thought that terrorism is a relatively new phenomenon in the world, but in point of fact terrorism did not begin with the Palestinians after the 1967 war, or in 1969 with the violence in Northern Ireland, or in 1972 with the Munich Olympics. Many Americans date terrorism from the 1993 attack on the World Trade Center, the 1995 Oklahoma City bombing of a government office building, or 9/11. The use of terrorism, however, goes back much, much further in time. One of the earliest examples of terrorism involved the efforts of Jewish extremists in the first century CE who used assassination and terrorism as a means of intimidating and silencing those in the Jewish community who were opposed to the idea of a revolt against being part of the Roman Empire. Supporters of the status quo and remaining in the empire were murdered in the streets of Jerusalem by members of groups supporting rebellion against Rome. Even though the revolt itself was eventually defeated by Roman legions, the initial terrorist campaign was quite successful in intimidating the pro-Roman elements into silence. When the revolt broke out, there was virtually no internal opposition.

The Reign of Terror in France, from which the term "terrorism" actually originated, is also an example of activities by radical groups, sometimes with the support of at least some of the leaders and factions active in the government of Revolutionary France, to use terrorism to achieve objectives. Thousands died at the hands of the government and mobs. The Boxer Rebellion in the late nineteenth century in China started out with terrorist attacks against European and Chinese Christians as part of their efforts to drive out foreign influences – even though it eventually became more of a conventional armed struggle against the European presence. These examples and others, including the Assassins discussed below, indicate that terrorism is anything but a new phenomenon. In fact, the use of terrorism by dissident groups has been present for many centuries.

THE ASSASSINS

Another early example of terrorism was the Islamic sect known as the Assassins. The Assassins were an unorthodox sect of Islam that appeared in the eleventh century. Because it was an unorthodox version of Islam, it adherents faced periodic persecution from other Muslim populations and their leaders. Even though we know about the Assassins because of a few attacks on Christian leaders in the

> The attacks against pro-Roman elements were quite effective. As Josephus (1987: 147), a Jewish writer who observed much of the violence noted, "More terrible than the crimes themselves was the fear they aroused." His observation would be equally descriptive of many modern terrorist groups.

crusader states in the Holy Land, the vast majority of their victims were fellow Muslims. Faced with continuing persecution from fellow Muslims and with limited military resources, the Assassins had to find another way to protect themselves.

The sect developed a twofold defensive policy to defend themselves. The first step was to occupy abandoned strongholds in the mountains of Persia and what is today Lebanon that provided safe havens for at least some members of the group. In addition, they began to assassinate the political leaders and officials of the states that were persecuting them. The group became quite adept in their assassinations. Despite the best efforts of the leaders to protect themselves, they were inevitably killed by members of the sect, and the assassins themselves usually died in the attempt. The death of the leaders and the willingness of the assassins to die demonstrated the power of the group to other political leaders. The assassinations usually occurred in public places so that the news of the deaths would spread throughout the population and to other states. Even in these days, there was an awareness of the importance of publicity for the target audience. At times the Assassins would send a warning (usually a dagger in the pillow of the leader or official) that would be sufficient to end any consideration of persecution. The result of this strategy of assassination was that the local rulers stopped persecuting members of the sect. The group as a political actor was eliminated during the course of the Mongol invasions in the last part of the thirteenth century. For more than two centuries, however, they had been quite successful in defending members of the sect from fellow Muslims, and, as a consequence, the group still exists today.

AL QAEDA AND THE GLOBAL JIHADISTS

No discussion of terrorism would be complete without a discussion of Al Qaeda. The group was initially formed in Pakistan by Osama bin Laden from among the foreign volunteers from many parts of the world who had come to fight against the Soviet occupation of Afghanistan. From the perspective of the members of Al Qaeda, the defeat of communism in Afghanistan represented the defeat of a Western ideology. First, there was the victory that came with the withdrawal of the military forces of the Soviet Union in 1989. Then, in 1992 the local Afghan communist regime in the capital was eliminated. After these victories Al Qaeda began to turn its attention to other aspects of Western culture and ideas that had penetrated the Middle East and other Islamic countries. In the view of Al Qaeda and its members, these Western influences threatened the traditional religious and cultural values of these societies. The United States in particular symbolized the evils present in Western culture and society and the ongoing changes within Islamic society because it was the leading Western power. The United States also became a target because it supported Middle Eastern governments where the rulers favored more secular ideas and therefore were not Islamic enough. These governments supported by the United States were authoritarian ones as well. When the United States sent military forces to protect Saudi Arabia after Iraq invaded Kuwait in 1990, bin Laden felt that Muslims were disgraced because they were no longer capable of defending the holy cities of Mecca and Medina. Finally, bin Laden opposed the United States since it had become conspicuous for its support for Israel in its confrontations with the Arab countries and the Palestinians in the Occupied Territories. His opposition became clear in 1998 when he issued a fatwa (religious pronouncement) that called on good Muslims to kill Americans at any time or place in the world.

Before the attacks of 9/11, Al Qaeda was a more hierarchical organization at its core with bin Laden as the leader and key lieutenants in lower level positions of authority. Even in its early days, however, there was a great deal of flexibility in the organization. The central leadership planned some operations directly. In other cases, the group relied on links with relatively autonomous organizations in different countries to carry out operations. Finally, in some circumstances, Al Qaeda would provide financial and technical support for groups that planned their own operations that were in keeping with the general goals of Al Qaeda. The attacks on 9/11 were the prime example of direct planning. The attacks on the US embassies in Kenya and Tanzania in 1998 were basically carried out by an Egyptian group with direct links to Al Qaeda. The first attack on the World Trade Center in 1993 is an example where financial and technical support was provided to an independent group that conceptualized and carried out the operation.

The successful attack on the World Trade Center towers and the Pentagon in 2001 led to a change in the organizational structure of Al Qaeda. The invasion of Afghanistan removed the safe base for bin Laden and Al Qaeda that the Taliban had previously provided. The old semi-hierarchical nature of the organization had become more dangerous to the group and impossible to maintain. Al Qaeda has evolved into a much more decentralized structure and has become a major actor in a loose network, relying on a leaderless resistance style of operations. The national dissident groups operating in different countries that had maintained links to the old Al Qaeda were well placed to continue operations on their own initiative. In addition, new groups have appeared drawing their inspiration from Al Qaeda but lacking any formal or even informal connections with the organization. In the modern world Islamic militants continue to pursue political goals such as the creation of more Islamic governments in their home countries or combating the influence of the United States and the West. Smaller groups and individuals who believe in reducing the evils of Western influence and the spread of secular practices in their societies that come with modernization have also appeared. They have been able to participate in the broader struggle by attaching themselves and their actions to a larger movement.

The global jihad movement has proven to be quite effective in mounting attacks. This movement cannot be dismembered from the top since there is no core leadership that is essential for the continuation of the movement. If one of the individual cells is broken up by security forces, other cells and individuals remain immune to capture. Even as some individuals are caught, new groups can appear that link themselves to the global jihad and participate in the struggle against the West and the United States. Al Qaeda has become an example of leaderless resistance with the basic organization providing an example and inspiration for individuals and small groups around the world. This global jihadist movement will continue into the immediate future even if Osama bin Laden is killed or captured and Al Qaeda as an organization is completely dismantled. The context for violent activity has already been established for new militants and groups to attach themselves to the idea of combating global trends of modernization, Westernization, secularism, and change.

THE IRISH REPUBLICAN ARMY

The Irish Republican Army (IRA) has been in existence for more than ninety years. Although it has often been viewed as a Catholic dissident group fighting against Protestants in Northern Ireland, religion is only part of the differences between the dissidents and the local political system that has led to violence. The battle has also been between Irish nationalists and the Protestants in Northern Ireland who consider themselves to be British. Of course, the Irish nationalists are largely Catholic while the British are largely Protestant. The Irish Republican Army (IRA) first appeared in the aftermath of the 1916 Easter uprising in Dublin. It fought against the British control of the whole island until the British were convinced to grant effective independence to the Irish Free State in 1922. Some members of the IRA, however, were unhappy with the treaty that left Northern Ireland under British control and launched attacks against the new Irish government. This campaign was eventually defeated by the new Irish army. These members of the IRA also attempted to continue the struggle against the British in Northern Ireland but it was not successful. While the IRA was defeated at this time, it kept up intermittent violent attempts to drive the British out of Northern Ireland before 1970, but these efforts failed.

By the late 1960s tensions in Northern Ireland were increasing because the Catholic population was facing discrimination by the Protestant majority who kept the Catholic population in second class status. There were peaceful efforts, including marches and demonstrations, to gain more equality for the Catholics, but the Protestants generally were unwilling to make any concessions. The situation steadily deteriorated, and violence by the IRA against Protestants continued, and repression by the authorities increased. At this time the official IRA organization argued that violence was not going to be effective, and for the most part refused to take up arms. The more hard-line individuals split from the organization and created the Provisional IRA (the Provos). The Provos argued for using the same tactics as the IRA had used to help win independence. Over the course of time, the Official IRA disappeared, and the Provos came to be the IRA.

The struggle over Northern Ireland continued for many decades. The IRA and other militants attacked Protestants and representatives of the British government. There was violence by members of Protestant paramilitary groups who targeted the Catholic population in retaliation for the IRA attacks on Protestants. During the course of the violence the IRA mounted some spectacular attacks against the British in Northern Ireland and Britain. There were bombings against British army bases on the British mainland, the assassination of Lord Mountbatten (a distant relative of Queen Elizabeth II), and a bomb exploded in the hotel in Brighton where Prime Minister Margaret Thatcher was staying during the Conservative Party Conference in 1984. There was a remote control mortar attack against Number 10 Downing Street and Prime Minister John Major in 1991. Even though the British police and military were able to arrest many suspected IRA members, they could not defeat the organization.

Over the years there were a variety of efforts to end the conflict. There were ceasefires proclaimed by the IRA and attempts by the British government to increase the representation of Catholics in the local political institutions and to gain more equal rights. Eventually, the British and political spokespersons for the IRA were able to reach an agreement that appears to have ended more than thirty years of violence, granting more rights to the Catholics and accepting the eventual possibility of Northern Ireland uniting with the Republic of Ireland. The movement towards peace has led to new splinter groups that were opposed to the negotiations and anything less than the total incorporation of Northern Ireland into the Republic of Ireland. Hard-line members of the IRA left the organization after the agreements to oppose the continued British presence in Northern Ireland. They formed the Continuity IRA and the Real IRA as groups that wanted to continue the struggle, but they appear to have attracted only limited support. Their appearance, however, does indicate some of the difficulties that are present in ending long-lasting terrorist campaigns. Although the

IRA had become dormant by 2010, it has not disappeared and could reactivate if political tensions in Northern Ireland were to increase.

HIZBALLAH

Hizballah (the Party of God) appeared in Lebanon in the early 1980s. It appeared as a movement linked with the Shia population in Lebanon in the later stages of the ongoing civil war that had devastated that country. Domestically it represented the interests of the Shia Muslims, who are the largest group in the country but also the poorest on average. It eventually came to be the most important political group representing Shia interests. It benefited from support from the clerics ruling in the Islamic Republic of Iran that were quite willing to provide assistance to another Shia population. Hizballah has had both domestic and foreign political goals, but the domestic objectives have been more important in many respects to the organization.

Militants from Hizballah have attacked foreign troops on Lebanese soil. Suicide attacks against American marines and French paratroopers in 1983 were instrumental in leading to the withdrawal of the foreign peacekeeping forces from the Beirut area. Guerrilla and terrorist attacks against Israeli troops elsewhere in Lebanon contributed to the eventual withdrawal of these forces from most of Lebanon. Israel even eventually withdrew from a small area of southern Lebanon that had long been under effective Israeli control through proxy Lebanese forces from 1982 to 2000. All of these attacks were directed against foreign involvement, and they were related to the basic domestic concern of removing at least some foreign troops from the country.

Hizballah was also willing to use violence against domestic opponents in the struggles for political advantage in Lebanon, relying both on terrorist violence and like other political groups in Lebanon on its own militia. As the Lebanese political system began to rebuild itself, Hizballah became an important domestic political party like other Lebanese parties and a power to be considered. It also spent considerable time and effort on achieving domestic programs that benefited the Shia population in the country. The party also developed a wing that provided social services to the

Shia population. These actions and programs generated a great deal of political support in the Shia population that has meant that Hizballah has been an important participant in elections and the national legislature.

Hizballah has been primarily interested in the domestic political system. Like most Arab parties, however, it supports the Palestinians in their struggle for an independent state in areas occupied by Israel. It has provided assistance to groups in Gaza and the West Bank that have opposed the Israeli occupation and even the existence of Israel. It has, however, intermittently involved itself in actions directed against Israel, including rocket attacks, support for terrorism inside Israel, and incursions across the border against Israel, including rocket attacks and kidnappings of Israeli troops. While these actions are evidence of Hizballah's support for the Palestinian cause, they are also very popular with the Lebanese public. The confrontation with Israel in 2008 began with the death of three Israeli soldiers and the kidnapping of two others in a Hizballah attack. This action led to Hizballah rocket attacks and Israeli air and artillery strikes and the advance of Israeli ground forces into Lebanon. The military action increased Hizballah's support because it was able to continue its rocket attacks and to prevent Israel from destroying its military capabilities. The anger in Lebanon over the destruction from the Israeli attacks was generally directed against Israel for the nature of it retaliation against Lebanon and not against Hizballah for provoking the actions. The Israeli retaliatory strikes ultimately did not prove to be an effective counterterrorism or counter guerrilla technique.

THE KU KLUX KLAN

At the end of the American Civil War, the newly freed slaves in the southern states now had the right to vote and participate in government while many of the whites could not participate because of their service in the rebel government or armed forces. The Ku Klux Klan (KKK) appeared in 1867 and used terrorism to intimidate the former slaves and help the old elite regain control of the state governments. The freed slaves and their white supporters were assaulted, terrorized, and killed. The terror attacks were ultimately very successful in changing the balance of political forces. Once the white population was securely in control, the KKK disbanded since it was no longer needed.

The KKK reappeared in the 1920s, but it had a different political agenda. While it was still anti-black, black Americans were second class citizens and the KKK was not necessary as a means of controlling a minority. It was more concerned with immigrant groups from southern and eastern Europe. The new immigrants were culturally different and overwhelmingly Jewish or Catholic, both of which were suspect religions for the KKK which was overwhelmingly Protestant. Various local branches of the KKK used violence against the new immigrants in efforts to preserve the privileged position of the white, Anglo-Saxon, Protestant population. It is not a coincidence that US immigration quotas were established at this time, and the quotas discriminated against migrants from southern and eastern Europe. The KKK eventually faded in the years prior to World War II, but it never disappeared completely.

The KKK resurfaced in the southern United States in the 1950s and 1960s with the advent of the civil rights movement. It used violence and terrorism in these efforts to defeat the campaign to provide equal rights for black Americans. It failed in its efforts, in part because the FBI and other police agencies were able to infiltrate the various branches with relative ease. While the KKK was defeated and as an organization was greatly weakened, other groups appeared to take its place. Groups like the Aryan Nations continued the animosity against minority groups, including black Americans, Jewish citizens, and members of immigrant groups from different cultural areas such as the Middle East and Asia. There have also been sporadic attacks against members of these different minorities. Many of these new racist, anti-immigrant groups have operated within the context of leaderless resistance types of networks.

The anti-immigrant groups in the United States have their counterparts in Europe. A variety of groups have appeared that have been opposed to immigrant communities, especially those from culturally different areas of the world such as Asia, parts of Latin America, Africa, or the Middle East. The migrants consist of guest workers, refugees from conflicts, or asylum seekers. The opposition to the presence of these communities has increased when the migrants were Muslim, Hindu, or from other non-Christian traditions. The anti-immigrant groups in question are not particularly religious, but they were opposed to these "foreign" religions. As was the case in the United States, the groups have launched attacks against those that they dislike in efforts to drive them out. There have been increasing contracts between such groups in Europe and the United States, perhaps in part because the European groups have become increasingly concerned about minorities and immigrants. Many of the migrants have faced at least verbal harassment and a significant number have experienced physical assaults. Muslim groups have become especially suspect after the 9/11 attacks, the Madrid train bombings in 2004, and the London transport bombings in 2005.

EUZKADI TA ASKATASUNA (ETA)

Euzkadi ta Askatasuna (ETA), or Basque Homeland and Freedom, is a Basque nationalist group that was formed in the 1970s while Francisco Franco was still ruling in Spain. Before the Spanish Civil War of 1938–1939, the Basque region had a significant degree of local autonomy. This autonomy was lost with the victory of Franco and the Nationalists. The Basque region sided with the Republicans during the Civil War, but the Franco regime was also in favor of government centralization. The founders of ETA sought to reverse this process and regain autonomy for the region or even to gain independence. The group launched a small number of attacks in the last years of the Franco regime. The targets usually were government officials and members of the Civil Guard (a national paramilitary police unit). Their most spectacular action occurred

Migrants from other areas of the world have faced problems in many European countries. In Sweden migrants from Asia, Africa, and Latin America have been targeted. In one year, one of seven men were subject to a physical assault and as many as half the non-European immigrants have been threatened, harassed, or assaulted. (Bjorgo 1997: 42) when a bomb planted in a tunnel under a street detonated and killed the prime minister as he was being driven down the street.

With the advent of a democratic system in Spain, ETA continued its terrorist activities. It was able to increase its attacks since there were more limitations on the security forces and more rights for those suspected of being involved in any attacks. ETA has continued to be active into the twenty-first century, and still hopes to achieve independence for the Basque areas of Spain and even in theory the Basque areas of France. There were a number of political parties that appeared in the Basque region, seeking greater autonomy or independence. The most extreme nationalist party, Herri Batsuna, in effect served as the political arm of ETA. Although any direct link between the two has always been denied, the party was banned in 2003 for providing financial support to ETA.

Through the more than quarter of a century of its existence, ETA adopted a wide variety of techniques. There were continuing attacks against government officials. At one point ETA undertook a rather effective campaign to disrupt the Spanish tourist industry by bombing hotels on the Mediterranean coast. The group also on occasion attacked wealthy Basque businesspeople to encourage financial contributions to the independence cause. The violence by ETA has contributed to political changes important for the region. The central government has granted greater autonomy to the area. These concessions by the government have reduced support for ETA. Greater international cooperation between French and Spanish officials has also reduced, but not eliminated, the ability of ETA to continue its attacks. There have been talks between representatives of ETA and the Spanish government, and ETA has accepted ceasefires for periods of time, but the group still continues to fight for independence for the Basque homeland.

THE NAXALITES

The Naxalites were a Marxist-Leninist groups that appeared in the Bengal area of India in 1967. The West Bengal state, which includes Calcutta, was a stronghold for leftist parties. There were two communist parties in the state – one that was aligned with the Soviet Union and one that was aligned with China. Both parties frequently served in governing coalitions. A third communist party appeared, drawing its members from the two parties. These members were dissatisfied with the slow pace of change in government policies that left the poorer members of society in virtually the same position as before. The new party was particularly active in rural areas where peasant families and other locals were losing control of their land to large landowners.

The Naxalites derived their name from the village of Naxalbari where violence broke out. Local conditions in the village and the surrounding area were particularly difficult. Landlords were gaining control of more and more land. As disputes between the landlords and the peasants increased, the landlords formed gangs to intimidate the peasants. The landlords were able to use their resources to influence the local police and government officials. The courts were frequently used by the landlords. When the courts ruled in favor of the peasants, the writs were not enforced, and when criminal charges were brought against the landlords or their employees, the defendants were often acquitted (Banerjee 1984: 86, 103). In this situation, the Naxalites began to use violence to pressure the landlords and others to treat the poorer inhabitants better. Assaults and property attacks were effective in getting better treatment for the peasants. As the local dissidents began to make progress in the area, the Indian government sent in police reinforcements even military units that were successful in defeating the dissidents and driving them into more inhospitable areas.

While the initial violence activity by the leftists was dealt with by the government forces, they were not completely eliminated. More importantly, the government did nothing to reform the local conditions that had led to the appearance of the violent dissidents. The Naxalites were able to recover and to once again become a political force in the region. By 2010 the violence had become more deadly. The dissidents were able to mount major attacks on police stations, killing a number of officers. The attacks proved to be a major embarrassment to the government which had thought that it had the situation under control.

One other reason why the group was able to recover and become dangerous again was because there were other outbreaks of violence throughout India. Violence by different leftist groups came to be known by the generic term Naxalite, even though many of the groups had no direct connection to the dissident group in West Bengal. The presence of the other groups plus government concern with other types of violence in the country, problems in Kashmir, and continuing tension with Pakistan meant that Indiansecurity forces were stretched thin. The problems that India has faced with the Naxalites and other leftist groups has clearly shown that violence and terrorism by leftist groups has not disappeared from the world with the collapse of the Soviet Union and negative publicity on communist governments. Leftist terrorist groups still exist and find support.

THE TAMIL TIGERS

The Tamil Tigers were formed in Sri Lanka to defend the interests of the Tamil minority in that country. Under British colonial rule the Tamils had become overrepresented in the professions and the civil service. When Sri Lanka became an independent country, political parties representing the Sinhalese majority began to establish quotas on the positions that the Tamils could have in the professions, universities, and government service. Sinhalese was made the official language and Buddhism the official religion of the country. Most Tamils did not speak Sinhalese, and they were either Hindu or Christians; therefore, the intent of the majority to disadvantage the Tamils was obvious. In 1983 there were riots that targeted the Tamils after an insurgent group attacked an army patrol and killed a number of soldiers. Mobs attacked Tamils and Tamil cultural sites. Between 2,000 and 3,000 Tamils died in the violence, and more than 100,000 became refugees. During the violence, the police did little to protect the Tamils or their property (Kaarthikeyan 2005: 134). In the aftermath of these mob actions, many dissident Tamil groups appeared using violence to seek changes in policies, autonomy for the Tamil areas within a federal system, or complete independence for the Tamil regions of the country. The Tamil Tigers (or the Liberation Tigers of Tamil Eelam) eventually became the dominant Tamil dissident group. They took a more extreme view, pushing for independence rather than autonomy or equal rights, although at times they appeared willing to bargain over the future. The Tamil Tigers absorbed some of the other dissident groups while other competing groups were eliminated by force.

The Tigers used terrorism, guerrilla attacks, and even became involved in larger scale battles with the Sri Lankan armed forces. The terrorist attacks were launched against a variety of targets, including high level government officials, security personal, bureaucrats, and the Sinhalese population in general. The group was also responsible for a large number of suicide attacks. The Tigers eventually became strong enough to control large areas of the country and to engage in a civil war against the government. The Tigers were able to hold their own against the Sri Lankan armed forces for many years. The Tigers also became involved in combat with Indian peacekeeping forces that were sent to the country in an effort to resolve the conflict. The Indian efforts failed, and the military forces were withdrawn.

The Tigers were finally defeated in 2009 after more than twenty-five years of struggle by the Sri Lankan armed forces. The tide in the long battle may have turned against the Tamil Tigers when the tsunami set off by an underwater earthquake in 2004 hit Sri Lanka. The areas of the country most heavily affected by the tsunami included the regions of the country controlled by the Tigers in the east and the north of the island. Although the government and the Tigers agreed to a truce during the rescue and recovery operations, the fighting eventually resumed. The government forces were now able to gain the upper hand since the government had the resources to recover more quickly from the results of the natural disaster, and the Tigers were then completely defeated.

Between 1980 and 2003 the Tamil Tigers were involved in more suicide attacks than any other single group and more attacks than all the Palestinian groups combined. (Lutz and Lutz 2008: 74–6)

ZIMBABWE UNDER MUGABE

The last example is one of government supported terrorism rather than violence by a dissident group. Robert Mugabe came to power in Zimbabwe after a successful guerrilla struggle led to majority rule by the African population in the former Rhodesia that had been governed by a white settler minority. Mugabe won the first election in 1979 that was part of the arrangements for independence in 1980, but he soon began to use repression against opposition political groups and the general population in regions that were strongholds of the opposition parties. Zimbabwe became for all practical purposes a one party state for many years.

Under Mugabe's leadership, Zimbabwe began to experience major economic difficulties and a marked decline in standards of living. The government was also afflicted with increasing levels of corruption that contributed to the national economic problems. One consequence of the declining economic situations was the end of subsidies that had previously been paid to the veterans of the guerrilla struggle. The veterans then focused on some of the commercial farms that were still owned by whites. The veterans began squatting on the farms and started confrontations with the owners in efforts to take over the farms that they regarded as a remnant of colonialism and rule by the white settlers. The confrontations became increasingly violent. The police were instructed not to respond to calls from the white farmers for assistance in protecting their property. Writs issued by the courts in favor of the farmers were not enforced. In confrontations resulting in injuries or death, only the whites were prosecuted. The ongoing process represented terrorism by private groups that were initially tolerated by the government and at times actively supported by the government. Most of the white farmers eventually gave up their farms and left the country. Those that remained even in the face of the violence lost their farms when they were eventually taken over by the government and distributed to the veterans.

The white farmers were more vulnerable to terrorism supported by the state because they had, quite naturally, favored a new opposition party that had appeared. Since the attacks against the farmers had worked, the same techniques were used against this party. Some repressive actions were undertaken by the police or security forces, but many more actions were launched by members of the government party, the party militia, or a youth wing of the party. Supporters of the opposition were assaulted or killed. Other members, including candidates for political office, simply disappeared. Rallies for the party were disrupted by either the police or by party groups. As had been the case with the white farmers, when there were confrontations that became violent the only persons ever arrested were members of the opposition. Even with the increased government repression and the terrorist violence, the new party mounted an effective election campaign in 2008. Its presidential candidate finished slightly ahead of Mugabe in the first round of voting but faced a runoff since he had not won a clear majority. The candidate eventually withdrew from the runoff election because of the dangers to his supporters. As a consequence, Mugabe was able to begin another term as president.

The government support for the terrorism against its own citizens in Zimbabwe is evidence of the weakness of the government. Mugabe's government did not launch the attacks against the white farmers on its own. It appears that it was unable to control the veterans, and it chose to support their violence rather than attempt to control or direct them. Attempts to stop the violence could have provoked a reaction that might have resulted in attacks against the government and the ruling elite. The white farmers provided a useful diversion for a group of potentially dangerous party militants. With the new opposition party, government repression alone was no longer working, so additional violence was required to keep the opposition in check. For the moment, this combination of repression and government supported terrorism has kept the old political elite in power.

CONCLUSIONS

The above examples are just a sample of the terrorist organizations that have been active. The examples represent groups with religious, ethnic, and ideological motives and goals and some with mixtures of motivations. The efforts of Mugabe to stay in power, however, may largely have reflected a desire of the political elite to continue to enjoy the privileges of office. The situation in India with the Naxalites also involved some state toleration of violence by the landlords. There are, of course, many more such groups that have been active in the twentieth and twenty-first centuries. While most groups have had little impact, the organizations above are not the only examples of groups that have made their presence felt.

KEY TERMS

Assassins, Euzkadi ta Askatasuna, Hizballah, Irish Republican Army, Ku Klux Klan, Naxalites, Al Qaeda, Tamil Tigers

FURTHER READING

Lutz, J. M. and B. J. Lutz (2008) *Global Terrorism*, 2nd edn, London: Routledge.

This introductory volume contains case studies on the above groups and many others that provide a useful base for evaluating terrorist groups. The volume also includes and extensive bibliography with additional sources on many groups.

WILL TERRORISM CONTINUE?

There is little doubt that terrorism will continue to be a problem in many parts of the world. There are a number of reasons why attacks will continue, perhaps at a decreasing rate or perhaps at an increasing rate. They will continue, however, despite the various counterterrorism techniques that are available to governments and the increasing level of resources devoted to defeating terrorist organizations. They will continue even if governments find the right mix of defensive techniques. The reasons for the continued use of terrorism by dissident organizations and governments include the fact that terrorism has worked in the past to achieve major objectives. Terrorism has also been effective in terms of achieving some intermediate goals for organizations. Terrorism is also a violent technique that is an inexpensive one, which requires relatively few resources. Related to the cost effective nature of terrorism is the fact that this type of violence remains a weapon of the weak.

HOW SUCCESSFUL IS TERRORISM?

As already noted, most terrorist groups fail very quickly as their members are apprehended by the police or as the member become discouraged by the lack of progress in the struggle against the governments and by the dangers involved. In fact, there have been suggestions that terrorism is virtually doomed to fail in terms of achieving any long-term or even intermediate objectives. This suggestion, however, appears to be an exaggerated view. There are a number of fairly obvious examples of successes achieved by the use of terrorism. One obvious area where terrorism has been successful involves those cases where the state uses terrorism as noted in

Chapter 6. Of course, state terrorism or state supported terrorism has greater chances of success and is something of a special case. State terrorism even when employed by a weak state has a chance of attaining political objectives. Mugabe and his colleagues have managed to stay in power in Zimbabwe through a combination of terror and repression. While not all state uses of terrorism will be successful, they do provide examples of success. Many of those who argue that terrorism is likely to fail do not include state terrorism, and dissident terrorism is much more prevalent.

Most cases of terrorism, however, involve dissident groups, but even some of these groups have been successful as well. National liberation movements involved in anti-colonial struggles have achieved their key objective of independence. The British gave up the struggle to control most of Ireland when the Irish Free State was established in 1922. The British also left Palestine in 1948 and Cyprus in 1960. The French pulled out of Algeria in 1962. The dissidents in Algeria relied on both terrorism and guerrilla warfare. In Cyprus there was some guerrilla activity that supported a major terrorist campaign in the urban areas against British officials and local Cypriot supporters. In the case of Ireland and Palestine, the dissidents relied on terrorism to accomplish their goals, and neither struggle ever reached the stage of active guerrilla warfare. Such colonial situations provide a number of advantages for the nationalists. There is likely to be a divide between the ruling authorities and the general colonial population that the dissidents can utilize. The governing colonial power had someplace to go when they agreed to independence. Even the well-established settler population in Algeria had the option of returning to France – as most of them did when it became clear that Algeria was going to gain its independence.

There have been other examples of success that have largely gone unnoticed. In the 1920s and 1930s, there were violent dissident movements, which were seeking to create independent Croatian and Macedonian states out of the Kingdom of Yugoslavia. The Croats had been rather enthusiastic supporters of the idea of Yugoslavia after World War I, but they quickly came to dislike the dominance of the new state by the Serb political elite. The Macedonians were similarly disillusioned. Both groups had nationalist organizations that used terrorist attacks as part of their efforts to create new states, but they were unsuccessful except for the brief creation of a puppet Croatia by Nazi Germany during World War II that was governed by a local fascist party. With the end of World War II, the idea of an independent Croatia disappeared. These independence movements failed at the time, and they would normally be considered examples of movements that had failed to achieve their basic goals. There were sporadic attacks by Croat nationalists in the 1960s and 1970s in Europe and North America that tried to draw attention to the goal of an independent Croatia, but they had little effect. Yet, if one looks at a map of Europe today, there is currently an independent Croatia as well as an independent Macedonia. It is quite possible that the violent efforts before World War II to create these independent countries kept alive the concept of independent states. The actions after World War II by the Croat nationalists may have had a similar effect. It is possible that because of these earlier terrorist efforts, both Croatia and Macedonia were able to break away a half-century later when Yugoslavia was weak and vulnerable because the idea of independence had been kept alive.

The organizations discussed in Chapter 8 also provide examples of successful terrorism. The Assassins were quite adept at providing protection for the sect members. Centuries later the KKK was an important factor in the return to power of the old elite in the American South. While the old leaders might have eventually returned to power, there can be no doubt that the KKK at least sped up the process. Hizballah has been able to use terrorism in a very effective fashion. Not only have the attacks achieved goals such as forcing out foreign troops, but the actions helped to propel the organization into an important domestic political position.

There are more recent examples of successful campaigns by dissident organizations. In Nepal a leftist group used guerrilla warfare and terrorism to help bring about significant changes in the political system. The monarchy has lost much of its real power, and the government is now ruled by a prime minister and government that depend upon a popularly elected legislature. In 2010 the former rebels held seats in the national legislature and were part of the governing coalition cabinet. In Kosovo, the **Kosovo Liberation Army** campaigned to create an independent Kosovo

> Albanian dissidents seeking to separate Kosovo from what
> remained of Yugoslavia in the 1990s concluded that "you could
> win more by a few months of armed struggle than Albanian
> politicians had achieved in nearly a decade of peaceful politics"
> (Ash 2003: 63). There is, in fact, now an independent Kosovo.

free of Serb rule. Its actions played a role in the eventual creation of
an independent Kosovo that is now ruled by the majority Albanian
population. The members of this group felt that violence had been
an essential part of the successful effort to separate Kosovo from
what remained of Yugoslavia.

The IRA, PLO, and ETA have also been able to attain some of
their objectives. The IRA campaign after World War I was essential
in bringing about the creation of the Irish Free State, even if
Northern Ireland was not included. The campaigns of the IRA later
in Northern Ireland did not bring about the desired unification,
but there have been political changes in the north that have been
favorable to the Catholic population. In the case of the PLO, Israel
eventually proved willing to negotiate with the organization as the
representative of the Palestinians in the Gaza Strip and the West
Bank. Under the Oslo Accords the PLO and Israel agreed to the
creation of the Palestinian Authority for the Palestinians while
the PLO recognized Israel's right to exist. While there is still no
independent Palestinian state, it is at least a possibility that would
have been less likely without the activities of the PLO. In the case
of ETA, there is no independent Basque state at present, but the
Basque region in Spain has been granted considerable autonomy, a
situation that would not have been likely to have happened if ETA
had not been active.

INTERMEDIATE GOALS

Even though most terrorist organizations frequently have difficulties
in achieving their long-term objectives, some of them may be able
to have at least some partial successes and are able to achieve some
important intermediate goals. Some of these objectives may be

related to the outbidding, spoiling, and provocation strategies that were mentioned in previous chapters. Successes in these areas are likely to increase the probabilities of achieving some of the more long-term objectives of a terrorist organization.

Terrorist organizations are essentially political organizations that may be competing with other violent dissident groups for recruits, finances, and other forms of support. Even paramilitary or militia groups operating with the toleration or the active support of the government may be competing with each other. The groups, whether dissident or pro-government, that are perceived to be more successful will attract the resources. The leaders of the groups would see their actions as successful when they displace other factions seeking the same or similar goals. If a dissident group is able to appropriate the vast majority of the resources available to dissident groups opposed to the government, it is likely to be more effective. Although the specific group winning this battle for resources may not achieve its ultimate objectives, the intermediate step can contribute to later successes and strengthen the organization. It can also be argued that in most cases the chances of achieving objectives that are shared by a number of groups are more likely when competing dissident factions are eliminated and the resources are concentrated in a single organization. The Tamil Tigers managed to absorb or eliminate other dissident groups. Its ability to unify the opposition helps to explain its ability to maintain its campaign for independence for so long.

Dissidents can also adopt spoiling strategies that are designed to disrupt peace negotiations, elections, or other government projects. Groups may attempt to disrupt elections if they or their allies are unlikely to win. Islamic rebels in Algeria in the 1990s wanted to disrupt elections in part to weaken the government and lessen its legitimacy. The elections also provided a forum for more moderate Islamic leaders who might then be able to lead those who wanted change in the political system. A group may feel that it is essential to prevent peace negotiations that could undercut the goals of the organizations. A compromise peace might result in the end of support for the dissidents as formerly unhappy citizens become willing to accept the changes offered by the government. If concessions are likely to solve the dispute, the hardliners could be opposed to an agreement as was the case with the Real IRA and the Continuity IRA. Preventing such a negative outcome from the perspective of the group can also be important for the future positive prospects of the group – even if the organization is miscalculating its chances of ultimate success. The assassination of Prime Minister Yitzak Rabin in 1995 for being insufficiently protective of Israel by his willingness to compromise with the Palestinians prevented outcomes opposed by some in Israel. He was assassinated by a Jewish extremist who disagreed with giving up land in the West Bank. His death was an effective spoiling attack since the implementation of the Oslo Accords was slowed down and then effectively stillborn. The attack itself was not an isolated action since there had been other terrorist activities by Jewish extremists opposed to any concessions to the Palestinians. The assassination is an example of an individual act within a wider framework of the leaderless resistance campaign of terrorism designed to keep the West Bank as part of Israel.

Sometimes governments can undertake spoiling or provocative actions, such as when Ariel Sharon made a well-publicized visit with an armed guard to the Dome of the Rock, a very holy site for Muslims in Israel and the Occupied Territories as well as those in other countries. The riots that were a direct consequence of the visit were very effective in promoting election outcomes that favored those opposed to negotiations with the Palestinians, including Ariel Sharon and his party. If governments need to take a more clandestine approach, a paramilitary can be encouraged to undertake attacks that will derail negotiations. The attacks may be blamed on the dissidents who are charged with negotiating in bad faith. They can also be intended to provoke the dissidents into a violent reaction. If the attacks are made against supporters of the dissidents, the organization may feel obligated to strike back to protect its supporters. Violence may serve as an excuse to postpone an election in the interests of public safety (and thereby insure the continuation of the current government in power). Such attacks could also provide the government with an excuse not to follow through on concessions or to break off negations with dissidents. Such government involvement in spoiling attacks can obviously succeed. A disruption in negotiations may be productive from the government's perspective if it feels that it was being forced into making too many concessions or if it believes that the circumstances have changed so that a counterterrorism policy of outright repression is now likely to succeed.

Spoiling attacks may also be intended to indicate to the government that it cannot proceed with some policies without making some concessions to the dissident group. Sunni Arab terrorists in Iraq in the years after the 2003 invasion cannot hope to regain the position of overwhelming political dominance that they held for all the years prior to 2003. Their attacks have been intended to demonstrate to the other factions in Iraq that any government in Iraq is not going to be able to function if the interests of the Sunni Arab minority are ignored. This violence is basically a demonstration of negative power wherein concessions to the minority are necessary for stability and peace. The success of this type of terrorism needs to be evaluated not only in terms of what organizations seek to accomplish in a positive sense but in what they may be seeking to prevent. Negative goals can be the very essence of spoiling attacks.

Dissidents can undertake provocation strategies that are designed to provide important short term benefits to the organization. Attacks designed to provoke overreactions among the target audiences or their governments can be an intermediate objective. Many terrorist groups have been successful in getting governments to overreact with negative policy changes or with getting the security forces to adopt harsher measures for dealing with suspect populations, thus alienating them and leading them to provide active or at least tacit support to the dissidents. Limitations on civil liberties imposed by a government can play into the hands of the dissident groups. Guantanamo Bay, for example, has provided Al Qaeda and groups linked to the global jihad with a propaganda advantage. These groups and their supporters are able to portray the United States as anti-Islamic because it will not apply the civil liberties supposedly present in a democracy to Muslims. As a consequence, it becomes easier to recruit new members and to mobilize support for the continuing struggle between Islam and the West.

It is obvious that other dissident organizations at times intentionally sought to create similar overreactions by security

> Governments may be aware of the dangers of provocation. Plans for attacking Al Qaeda targets in Afghanistan in 1998 were put aside since the damage done might not justify the increased sympathy for Al Qaeda and the Taliban. (Benjamin and Simon 2002: 294–6).

forces. The Kosovo Liberation Army consciously attempted to force the Serbian military and security forces into adopting more repressive measures against the Albanian population by attacks on isolated police and military patrols. The police were especially targeted. The IRA was quite effective in pursuing such strategies with the British troops in Northern Ireland, driving a wedge between the Catholic community and the military. Many of the bombings in Iraq after 2003 have been intended to bring about crackdowns by the government or overreactions by other segments of Iraqi society. In all of these cases intermediate goals were achieved that may or may not have contributed to long-term successes. Organizations may miscalculate the long-term effects of their actions, the circumstances previously favorable to the dissidents may change, the government may receive important external assistance or find an effective counterterrorism policy, or the dissidents may make fatal mistakes. Even so, the intermediate successes can be important even if eventual victory will depend upon other events and circumstances.

Al Qaeda as an organization and the global jihad movement as the loosely connected network that has grown out of Al Qaeda, have utilized multiple strategies at various times that have included intermediate objectives. One of the initial goals sought by bin Laden and Al Qaeda with the early terrorist attacks such as the East African embassy attacks was an effort to drive a wedge between the United States – and the West in general – and the Muslims in the Middle East and elsewhere. The 9/11 attacks included this objective among others, and the US reaction to the attack suggests that Al Qaeda appears to have succeeded quite well with this goal. The response by the United States provided Al Qaeda and related groups with an opportunity to portray the

United States as launching attacks against Islam in general. Even though this was not the US policy, the appearance of such an intent has been a potent propaganda weapon for the extremists. While the 2001 invasion of Afghanistan was not especially popular among Muslims, it was accepted by many as a logical consequence of the 9/11 attacks. The 2003 invasion of Iraq, which occurred for a complex set of reasons but within the context of the US global war on terrorism, however, was not accepted by most Arabs or many non-Arab Muslims as an appropriate response. The invasion has made it possible for Al Qaeda and related groups to portray their continuing attacks on the United States and the West as part of a continuing battle between Islam and the West. Individuals can see themselves as defending their religion and their countries against Western encroachment and what they see as economic, political, and cultural imperialism. Being able to portray the attack in this fashion has spurred recruitment, financing of various organizations, and the activities of independent groups that have launched attacks because they see themselves as part of the global jihad against the West. It is not especially surprising that Al Qaeda and other groups have been able to find many volunteers to launch attacks in Iraq since 2003 against the United States, other foreign troops, and those Iraqis seen as collaborating with the United States. The 9/11 attacks thus eventually served the provocation goal quite well, accomplishing one of the basic objectives of Al Qaeda.

TERRORISM AS AN INEXPENSIVE METHOD

Another reason why terrorism will continue is that it is quite cost effective. It does not require major financial resources for dissidents to begin to use terrorism, even if the initial efforts become successful campaigns that will eventually require more resources. Of course, if organizations are successful, they are more likely to attract the necessary additional resources. They have to use outbidding strategies against other dissident factions, but the most successful groups will naturally attract the resources. Achieving intermediate goals may be very important in this regard. A number of attacks that caused significant casualties such as the Madrid train bombings, the London transport bombings, or the attack on the federal office building in Oklahoma City by Timothy McVeigh were inexpensive. None of these attacks required a major outlay of funds. In fact, in these three cases the attacks were financed by the participants. The attempted car bombing in Times Square in New York in 2010 is another example of a relatively inexpensive attempt. If the attacker had been a bit more sophisticated, the bomb would have caused considerable damage and significant casualties. In the case of suicide attacks, groups with larger memberships can rely on them if suicide attacks are acceptable to the organization, its members, its supporters, and potential supporters. Suicide attacks can be more damaging at lower cost than conventional attacks as noted in Chapter 4. As long as terrorism as a technique remains relatively inexpensive, it will continue to be used by dissident organizations. Organizing an armed rebellion or creating a political party to contest political campaigns by contrast is a much more expensive proposition although successful terrorism campaigns may set the stage for more open rebellion as occurred in Sri Lanka with the Tamil Tigers. The inexpensive nature of terrorism also helps to explain why the technique will be used by governments. Even if the government supported attacks fail, very little will have been lost in terms of resources (unless the source of the attacks are discovered and public support for the government declines greatly as a consequence).

TERRORISM AS A WEAPON OF THE WEAK

Because terrorism is a relatively inexpensive technique, it will continue to be used by organizations that are weak – either in an absolute sense or relative to their opponents. The Palestinians resorted to terrorism as their primary technique when it became obvious after the 1967 war that conventional warfare by Arab armies or guerrilla warfare by Palestinian groups was unlikely to result in the end of Israel or the establishment of an independent Palestinian state. The PLO as an organization was not a particularly weak political organization, especially when compared to many other dissident terrorist groups, but it was weak relative to the Israeli Defense Force and the Israeli security services. Most dissident groups, of course, are quite weak in an absolute sense;

therefore, terrorism becomes their preferred technique precisely because there is a lack of alternative acceptable courses of action.

The groups that have turned to terrorism are weak, and they usually lack other options for achieving their political objectives, at least initially. While terrorism often will fail to achieve any of the long-term objectives or even intermediate ones, it will remain one of the few means available that weak organizations can use in an attempt to bring about political change. Ineffective as terrorism may be for many groups, the alternative will be to give up and to do nothing. Terrorism at least provides a prospect, however limited, of change. If doing nothing appears to be unacceptable to dissidents then terrorism will be tried. As a consequence, dissidents that are desperate to achieve political changes and willing to take the risks involved with violent action will continue to engage in terrorism. Similarly, weaker governments facing threats from discontented citizens will also be tempted to support terrorism as a means of staying in power. Even if the government terrorism may fail, it at least provides an opportunity to avoid collapse.

CONCLUSIONS

For the above reasons, there is little doubt that many different terrorist organizations will continue to rely on terrorism. It is one of the few techniques available for weak groups that lack resources precisely because it is inexpensive. It will also remain a useful technique for organizations with more resources that are absolutely weak or relatively weak compared to their opponents. Governments that lack the resources to deal with their opponents through repression will also continue to be tempted to utilize paramilitary or other informal pro-government organizations to deal with what they see as dangerous internal opposition.

Of course, if terrorism always failed, the fact that it is a weapon of the weak and that it is inexpensive would have little meaning. What gives terrorism the status of a persistent phenomenon is that fact that it succeeds at least some of the time or at least that it *appears* to succeed. It seems obvious that at least some dissidents have achieved major objectives as was noted above. In addition, others have managed to attain significant intermediate goals even if they may eventually be defeated and disappear or be forced to compromise without achieving their ultimate objectives. Other groups will make a transition to guerrilla warfare or even open rebellion as they become stronger and have access to more domestic or foreign resources. All the examples of such success or even the perception that dissidents have been successful will fuel additional terrorist activities by new groups copying the old. The time line of group activities can also be important. By 2010 the Tamil Tigers would appear to have been totally defeated in their efforts to create an autonomous or independent Tamil homeland in Sri Lanka, although it is possible that in fifty years there will be such a state just as there are now independent countries of Croatia and Macedonia. Even if there is never such a state, for many of the twenty-five years the Tamil Tigers operated, they appeared to have a good chance of being successful. As a consequence, even though the Tigers were eventually defeated, their struggle served as a positive example or even an inspiration for many other dissidents. The effectiveness (or apparent effectiveness) of suicide attacks by the Tamil Tigers no doubt encouraged other dissidents to consider using such attacks. During the period when the organization was active, the apparent successes were more relevant than the ultimate failure.

Perception is also important in other ways. Many of the groups and individuals involved in the global jihad see the battle as a clash between the West and Islam. Outside observers who share this view as a main cultural conflict that has exacerbated tensions may see similar opportunities for driving wedges between different segments of their domestic societies or between other religions or global areas. The apparent success of the strategy of provocation might lead other groups to attempt a similar strategy. Even if the global jihad will eventually fail in all senses of the word, it will have inspired similar attempts along the way – which may in turn then be in the process of influencing yet others who are considering relying on terrorism. Apparent successes can begin a vicious cycle where each perception that a group has attained an objective or seems like it *might* attain its ultimate objectives then encourages even more terrorism.

> Perception can be as important as reality in explaining political phenomena. It can be the "image of success that recommends terrorism to groups who identify with the innovator." (Crenshaw 2003: 98)

There seems to be little doubt that terrorism will continue to be an ongoing phenomenon and problem in the world. It is an inexpensive weapon that can be used by weak organizations that lack alternative means of attempting to achieve political objectives. Weak groups can include governments that resort to terrorism and which can be successful in doing so. It is also a technique that provides at least a chance of achieving major goals for dissident organizations even if that chance is relatively small. Terrorism as a technique has somewhat higher probabilities of gaining intermediate objectives than ultimate goals. Finally, there are obvious cases where particular terrorists appear to be having successes at the time, thus further encouraging adoption of terrorism as a method by other groups or governments.

KEY TERMS

Kosovo Liberation Army, Al Qaeda, Tamil Tigers

FURTHER READING

Abrams, M. (2006) "Why Terrorism Does Not Work," *International Security*, 31, 2: 42–78.

Abrams argues on the basis of a study of twenty-three groups that terrorist groups do not attain any of their key objectives and usually fail to even attain any tactical or short-term objectives.

Cronin, A. K. (2009) *How Terrorism Ends: Understanding the Decline and Demise of Terrorist Campaigns*, Princeton, NJ: Princeton University Press.

In discussing how terrorist groups can end, Cronin discusses examples of success and examples of transformation from terrorist activities to other types of political pressure that have been facilitated by the terrorist activities.

Lutz, J. M. and B. J. Lutz (2009) "How Successful Is Terrorism?" Forum on Public Policy, http://forumonpublicpolicy.com/spring09papers/papers09spring.html, 1–22.

The authors provide a fair number of examples of terrorist groups that achieved some of their basic goals and others that achieved some of their intermediate goals.

OVERVIEW

The preceding chapters have discussed many of the characteristics of terrorism and active groups. There have been a great many terrorist organizations that have operated in the world. Different types of terrorist groups continue to operate. While much of the current attention is naturally given to Islamic groups, there are many other types of terrorist groups. There are terrorists linked to other religions, and terrorists from ethnic groups have also not disappeared. Right-wing groups continue to operate in the United States and Europe, and even some leftist groups remain active as is the case with the Naxalites in India. Over the course of time, terrorist organizations that have several types of objectives have appeared in many parts of the world. Even though it is true that many terrorist groups fail quickly, some survive to become meaningful threats. This concluding chapter on the overview of terrorism will summarize the key findings from the earlier chapters, but first there will be a reevaluation of the factors that have been considered to be causes of terrorism or that contribute to terrorism.

ROOTS OF TERRORISM REEVALUATED

As noted in Chapter 2, there are a number of potential causes of terrorism. It is necessary to reemphasize that terrorism is simply a technique that is available for use by all kinds of groups with all kinds of grievances. The most obvious factor that leads to terrorism is that some portion of society becomes discontented enough to resort to violence. Any attempt to specify causes, however, must go beyond this basic fact. There will always be some obvious factors or circumstances that would lead dissidents or governments to resort to violence as a way of dealing with problems. It is also important to remember that terrorism is only one type of political violence. The same conditions and situations that lead to terrorism can also lead to other types of political violence. As noted earlier, discontented groups resort to terrorism when they cannot rely on political parties and elections, pressures groups, bribery, military interventions, or armed insurrection to achieve their goals. There are no unique causes of terrorism, but whatever causes other types of political violence can also be behind terrorism.

A number of suggestions were put forward to explain the incidence of terrorism. While the idea that poverty is a basic cause has been popular, there is nothing in the preceding chapters to suggest that poverty has been a major factor. The IRA is one group whose history would provide some support for the poverty explanation. In 1916, the Irish were poorer than their English counterparts. Of course, anti-colonial movements typically involve such differences since the colonial power is inevitably richer than the colony. Although differences no doubt contribute to the desire to end the colonial status, other conditions explain outbreaks of anti-colonial violence of all kinds. In the case of Northern Ireland, the Catholic Irish community was clearly less well off than the Protestant British residents. The reforms undertaken by the British government recognized the disparity between the two groups and attempted to correct it. Other cases of terrorism provide less support. Hizballah did represent a poorer segment of Lebanese society, but the group's most obvious terrorist actions have been against foreign targets. The Basque region of Spain has been one of the more economically advanced and prosperous areas of the country. As a consequence, concessions by the government to the Basque region did not deal with questions of poverty, but with increased autonomy for the area. In other cases, such as the whites who joined the KKK and the Tamils in Sri Lanka, moreover, the terrorists were better off economically than the general population. With government terrorism, poverty is not an issue. The case of the Mugabe government in Zimbabwe is a good illustration since the government support of terrorism was designed to preserve a position of privilege for the ruling elite, not to gain one.

Limited political participation can be a contributing factor in the appearance of terrorism. It has obviously been important in anti-colonial struggles since participation for the colonial subjects is limited or non-existent. National liberation movements frequently seek greater representation for the colonial population as part of their broader demands. The IRA, ETA, and Tamil Tigers all saw themselves as being in this type of situation. The Catholic Irish were underrepresented in Northern Ireland, but the Tamils were included in the Sri Lankan political system as were the Basques once democracy was established in Spain. The underlying problem for the Basques, Tamils, and Irish Catholics in Northern Ireland was that they were outnumbered political minorities. Al Qaeda and the global jihadists also feel that their views are not being represented by governments in the Middle East or respected by governments in the West. It is not clear, however, that Al Qaeda and similar groups represent majority opinion even if they do speak for the discontent of an important number of Muslims. For Hizballah, greater participation for the Shia in Lebanese society and the political system was a prime concern. Participation for the Palestinians in the Occupied Territories was a secondary issue for Hizballah. Frequently, government tolerated or supported terrorism is intended to limit participation by the citizens who are being targeted. The KKK and similar groups in Europe and North America today have also been intent on limiting participation of the groups of which they did not approve. In the time frame in which the Assassins operated, participation was not a primary issue. For the Assassins, survival for the group was the priority concern.

Globalization and the modernization that goes with it do have relevance for the use of terrorism by many groups. Clearly, Al Qaeda and the global jihadists are fighting against the effects of globalization and the increase of Western influences in Islamic societies in the Middle East and elsewhere. The penetration of more traditional societies by businesses, governments, aid workers, and perhaps most importantly Western ideas and values have generated changes and threats. As traditional structures change, there are more anomic individuals who may support extremist groups that are promising to combat the unwanted changes. The Naxalites have mobilized support from groups that have been adversely affected by economic and social changes occurring as the rural areas became more integrated into the national system and even the broader global system. Even some nationalist struggles reflect the effects of globalization even if the members of the groups do not necessarily think of their struggles in these terms. In some ways the nationalists are reacting to threats to their cultures and societies that have come with increasing incorporation into the broader world that often result in the assimilation of local societies and the disappearance of local languages. The Basques and Irish have seen their societies changed by increased interactions with the broader world. Irish Gaelic and Basque as languages are being displaced by English and Spanish notwithstanding efforts to keep them alive. The KKK in the 1920s and the current extreme right-wing groups in the United States and Europe, which are anti-minority and anti-immigrant, are other examples of violent reactions to globalization and the accompanying migration patterns. In essence, they are attempting to reestablish an idealized version of the past when their societies were much less diverse. Hizballah, on the other hand, has shown no direct indications of being a reaction to globalization, nor, for example, have the Assassins, the Tamil Tigers, or Mugabe's government in Zimbabwe. While global attention may have placed at least a few restraints on government actions in countries such as Zimbabwe, the attention may also have meant that governments rely more on irregular forces and terrorism rather than on repression.

State weakness has clearly contributed to some outbreaks of terrorism. A weak state structure permits dissidents to create organizations and to survive the early, dangerous days when many groups are dismantled by the police or security forces. Hizballah gained strength in Lebanon during the long civil war and internal turmoil among domestic groups that was aggravated by the interventions of outside states. The Naxalites have taken advantage of local weaknesses in the Indian political systems, and they have managed to survive in part because the police and security forces have been insufficient to deal with the dissidents. The ETA gained strength when Spain was in transition from Franco to the new democratic system. The Assassins appeared in a time when there were many smaller states instead of a large empire which provided an environment where they could organize and survive. While it stands to reason that terrorist organizations can benefit from weak states, not all groups have appeared in such circumstances. The IRA and most of the extreme right-wing groups have not been facing weak states. In fact, they often have been opposing policies in well-established political systems. The government of Sri Lanka that the Tamil Tigers were fighting was not as strong as European governments, but it would not qualify as weak. Al Qaeda has not just focused its efforts on weak governments or opportune situations, but has also taken on powerful countries, including the United States. Finally, weakness comes into play as a characteristic of dissident groups and governments that resort to terrorism. Mugabe's government tolerated the land occupations of the veterans because it was too dangerous to attempt to challenge the war veterans, and it relied on state supported terrorism to deal with the increasing domestic opposition because it was too weak to rely on other mechanisms of repression.

In the final analysis, there is no single cause for terrorism since it is simply a violent technique that is chosen by groups with limited alternatives for dealing with political problems and for attaining different kinds of objectives. Globalization, inequality, lack of representation, weak governments, and other factors – some of which could be very specific to individual sets of circumstances – can play a role in generating the necessary conditions that will lead to or contribute to the use of terrorism. Some groups will use terrorism for other reasons that are essentially practical ones. Government elites, for example, can use terrorism as a means of staying in power. The Assassins used a well developed campaign of terrorism to protect their sect from extinction. In the future there may be new causes, or at least variations on the existing causes. New objectives or mixtures of objectives could occur as well. Thus, there will always be exceptions that cannot be explained by any one cause, even a complex mixture of the more standard causes.

CONCLUSIONS

There are some conclusions and insights about terrorism that can be derived from the preceding chapters. Terrorism can indeed have many causes like most other political phenomena. Violent groups have varying goals including religious, national, and ideological ones. They pursue policy changes, government changes, and boundary changes. There are multiple combinations of these various objectives, meaning that many situations are relatively unique. The goals of the dissidents will then affect the types of responses that governments may take in their efforts to combat the violence. Identifying the objectives of the groups and the possible causes that underlie their activities will help any government response to be effective – whether it be a government response to domestic dissidents or response by foreign governments to states using terrorism against its own citizens. The multiple causes, of course, require specific mixtures of approaches to attempt to deal with the presence of terrorism, and there is not even any standard response to particular types of terrorism.

Individuals who join terrorist organizations do not have any obvious characteristics beyond high levels of commitment to the cause. They do not have any identifiable psychological traits and are frequently representative of their broader communities in terms of economic, social, and educational characteristics. Dissident groups that attract these individuals use a variety of tactics and weapons. Often, the weapons are whatever can be obtained, and in rare cases they could even include weapons of mass destruction. The groups can choose a wide variety of targets. In fact, one advantage that terrorists have is their ability to choose from a number of different types of targets and the fact that one member of a target audience can be replaced by another. These circumstances effectively multiply the number of potential targets. Governments supporting or using terror have different sets of tactics, including death squads, that they can utilize. Their targets will, of course, be different in many cases than the targets of dissident groups. Both governments and dissidents can choose their targets and tactics in the context of a number of overall strategies. Strategies can include attrition, intimidation, provocation, spoiling, and outbidding as discussed in earlier chapters. Even though some tactics are more likely to be more useful for particular strategies, most tactics can be used with any of the strategies or mixtures of them.

In order for terrorists to gain any chance of success, they have to find support. There has to be some domestic support when the targets and objectives are domestic, otherwise the groups cannot survive unless it is a front for a foreign intelligence service. Dissident groups can become more deadly when they can attract foreign support from governments, sympathizers, or diaspora populations. The presence of such foreign support will affect the chances of success for the groups. While most terrorist groups fail completely, there are some cases where violent dissident organizations have been successful in achieving either major or intermediate objectives. These successes, or at least the appearance of success, will encourage other groups to adopt the same tactics to achieve their goals. Government terrorism, of course, is much more likely to be successful. State terror can become more lethal if the government can attract support from the governments of foreign allies.

When all is said and done, terrorism appears to work at least in some cases for groups that are desperate enough to adopt this technique. Terrorism, as a consequence, will continue in the future. The future terrorists of 2020 or 2025 may still be predominately religious (Christian, Muslim, Hindu, or others). They could also be nationalist or ideological. Violent dissident ethnic organizations have continued into the twenty-first century. Extreme right-wing ideological groups still remain active in many countries. It is even possible that left-wing ideologies could stage a revival as the memory of the failures of communism fade into the past. The Naxalites demonstrate that violent left-wing ideologies are still possible even though the end of communism in the Soviet Union and Eastern Europe discredited leftist movements to a large extent. Government terrorism can also continue to be present as a means of dealing with opponents. While the exact nature or objectives of the terrorist groups of the future is unknown, there seems to be little doubt that terrorism will continue. Leaderless resistance styles of organization combined with modern communication technologies will be especially difficult for governments to counteract. Even the most effective counterterrorism measures currently known will not always work, and groups that feel they have no alternatives to their current situation except to rely on violence will appear and continue to use terrorism as a technique to achieve their goals.

GLOSSARY

Abu Sayyaf group in the Philippines was formed by individuals who had served in Afghanistan fighting Soviet troops and the local communists. It is one of the groups attempting to gain independence for the Muslim areas of the country. The group has had intermittent links to Al Qaeda since it was formed.

Al Qaeda is a radical Islamic organization that seeks to reduce Western influence in the Middle East among other goals. It has launched some spectacular attacks, including the ones on 9/11, and inspired violence by other individuals and groups.

Anarchists were a group of left-wing idealists who operated in the late nineteenth century and early twentieth century. They assassinated rulers and government leaders in an attempt to bring about political change. They were an early example of leaderless resistance.

Anomie refers to a situation in which an individual finds himself or herself without a known social, economic or cultural structure that provides a framework for everyday action. Members of anomic groups can be a source of recruits for terrorist groups.

Anthrax is a poison that can be quite deadly, especially when inhaled in its powder form. While it can kill and make people sick, it is not contagious.

Aryan Nations is one of a number of extremist right-wing groups in the United States. It is quite racist and has targeted minorities and Jews because they are considered to be threats to the purity of the white race.

Attrition strategy is pursued by terrorist groups and is designed to wear down a government until it is willing to make concessions or even give in to the terrorist organization completely in order to end the violence and the costs of dealing with it.

Aum Shinrikyo was a Japanese religious cult that launched a sarin gas attack on the Tokyo subway in 1995. The attack attempted to prevent a government investigation into the group's activities.

Black widows are a group of Chechen women who became suicide bombers to protest the continued Russian occupation of the region. The women were willing to become suicide bombers in revenge for their husbands or other family members who had been killed by the Russian military or security forces.

CIA is the major intelligence agency of the United States that focuses on foreign operations and seeks to deal with foreign terrorist groups that target US interests abroad or in the United States.

Death squads are non-governmental groups that seek out opponents of a government to assassinate them to instill fear in a target audience. While the squads are not official government units, many of the members come from the military or security agencies. They normally have the support of the government.

Diaspora populations are members of ethnic groups that have migrated abroad who still identify with local populations in their homeland.

A dirty bomb is a conventional explosive device that contains radioactive materials that can potentially cause sickness in people who are exposed. In addition, it can contaminate the area affected by the explosion.

Ethnic cleansing occurs when violence and terror are used by governments or other groups to drive an ethnic or religious group out of a particular area.

Euzkadi ta Askatasuna (ETA) is a Basque movement that has used violence in its efforts to achieve independence for the Basque region of Spain.

Extradition occurs when one country requests the deportation of an individual from another country for trial for crimes that were committed in the requesting country.

False flag attacks occur when an organization launches attacks and attempts to have the blame attached to some other group.

Genocide occurs when a government or even a non-governmental group attempts to destroy an ethnic or religious group.

Globalization refers to the increasing connections among different societies and cultures around the world in terms of economic, social, political, and communication linkages.

Government terrorism occurs when the ruling government or state agencies support terrorist attacks against their own citizens by other domestic groups such as paramilitary organization, militias, death squads, or vigilantes.

Guantanamo Bay is a US naval base in Cuba that has been used to house terrorist suspects who have been captured abroad. The individuals sent to the base in many cases continue to be held indefinitely with no prospect of being charged or brought to trial. Others have been returned to their home governments for either release or imprisonment.

Intimidation strategies are used by terrorists and are directed toward target populations. It is designed to get them to withdraw their support from the government – or their support from an opposition group if the government is pursuing such a strategy.

The Irish Republican Army (IRA) was involved in the successful struggle to create an independent Irish state after World War I. It later was a key actor in the terrorist campaign to drive the British out of Northern Ireland and unite that territory with the Republic of Ireland in the south.

Janatha Vimukthi Peramuna is a leftist political party in Sri Lanka. At one time it launched a terrorist and guerrilla campaign against the government in an effort to take power, but the attempt failed.

The Japanese Red Army is a leftist group that appeared in Japan to oppose capitalism in that country and global capitalism. Members of the group have been involved in terrorist attacks in other countries in collaboration with other leftist groups.

The KGB was the major intelligence agency of the Soviet Union when it existed. It was involved in both foreign operations and in dealing with internal dissidents.

Kneecapping is the technique, apparently first developed by the Red Brigades in Italy, of approaching a target and shooting him in one or both knees rather than killing the target. The disabled victim served as a constant reminder of the power of the terrorist group.

The Kosovo Liberation Army appeared to fight for an independent Kosovo that would be controlled by the Albanian population of the territory.

The Ku Klux Klan (KKK) was a right-wing racist terrorist organization that appeared three times in the United States. After the Civil War it sought to put whites in power at the expense of freed slaves. In the 1920s it reappeared as anti-Catholic, anti-Jewish, anti-immigrant, and anti-black. It appeared once again in the 1950s and 1960s to oppose the civil rights movement.

Leaderless resistance refers to a style of operations where individuals or small groups that identify with some larger cause undertake violent actions to achieve the goals of a larger group. They do not act under the direct orders of someone in a larger group although websites can provide information about potential targets.

Left-wing ideologies focus on reducing inequality and hierarchy in domestic societies. Many left-wing ideologies draw upon ideas of Karl Marx and Vladimir Lenin.

The London transport bombings were attacks in 2005 by a group of Muslims in the United Kingdom who identified with the aims of Al Qaeda but apparently had no direct contact or instructions from Al Qaeda. The four individuals launched suicide attacks on subway trains and a bus.

The Madrid train bombings in 2004 were undertaken by a group associated with Al Qaeda to protest the presence of Spanish troops in Iraq. Nearly 200 people were killed and many more were injured when bombs went off in crowded commuter trains coming into the Spanish capital.

The Naxalites were a leftist group in India that tried to protect peasants and the poor in the countryside from exploitation by local landlords and local political authorities. The term has now come to be used in a more general way to describe a variety of violent leftist groups operating in many parts of India.

The 9/11 attacks were launched by Al Qaeda operatives in September of 2001. Hijacked airliners flew into each of the twin towers of the World Trade Center and the Pentagon. A fourth hijacked airliner was destined for the White House but did not reach its target when it crashed in western Pennsylvania.

The Order was a right-wing extremist group in the United States. Even though the group lasted a little more than a year, it successfully robbed banks and armored cars.

The Oslo Accords was an agreement between Israel and the Palestinian Liberation Organization designed to end the conflict between Israeli authorities and the Palestinians in the Gaza Strip and the West Bank. The agreement created the Palestinian Authority and provided for at least an element of self-rule for the Palestinians.

An outbidding strategy is one that is designed to gain resources, support, and recruits at the expense of other dissident groups. Terrorist organizations may seek to launch more spectacular attacks in order to gain these types of support.

The Popular Front for the Liberation of Palestine was a terrorist group seeking an independent Palestine that combined nationalism with Marxist-Leninist ideology. It has had a clear leftist ideological orientation, The PFLP viewed the problem of Palestine as a result of global capitalism.

A provocation strategy is one that is designed to get the government or its security forces to overreact to the actions of the dissident group. The dissidents hope that the overreaction will negatively affect a portion of the population that will then turn to supporting the terrorist group instead of the government.

The Red Army Faction (or Baader-Meinhof Gang) was a leftist group in West Germany in the 1970s and 1980s that was determined to undermine the government and the international capitalist system.

The Red Brigades was a leftist group in Italy in the 1970s and 1980s that mounted a serious challenge to the government before it was finally contained by the Italian authorities.

Rendition is a practice used by the United States of transferring suspects from the United States or other countries to allied or friendly countries where the security agencies can use torture to extract intelligence from the suspects.

The Revolutionary Armed Forces of Colombia (FARC) is a dissident leftist group that has been active for many years in Colombia. It has used both terrorism and guerrilla tactics and has gained control of some rural areas. It has developed a cooperative working arrangement with the drug cartels in Colombia.

Right-wing ideologies favor the status quo and often seek to return societies to an earlier time that is seen as an ideal period. Such groups are often opposed to immigrants from foreign cultures or religions.

Sarin gas is the nerve gas used by Aum Shinrikyo in its attacks against the passengers on the Tokyo subway. Although it can be deadly, the materials used in the subway attack were too weak to cause mass casualties.

The Secret Intelligence Service is the main intelligence agency of the United Kingdom dealing with foreign operations and foreign threats.

The 17 November Organization was left-wing terrorist group in Greece that managed to elude the security forces for a quarter of a century before a premature explosion of a bomb led to the exposure of the organization.

Shining Path was a leftist terrorist and guerrilla group active in Peru that controlled rural areas and which cooperated with drug producers.

A spoiling strategy is one that is designed to prevent what a terrorist group regards as a negative outcome. The strategy can be used in attempts to disrupt elections or peace negotiations.

Suspect communities are formed when governments or local populations begin to believe that members of the ethnic or religious groups are likely to be terrorists. As a consequence the group members are subjected to greater scrutiny or even discrimination.

The Symbionese Liberation Army was a small leftist group in California opposed to the American political and social system. Its major feat was the kidnapping of Patty Hearst and her apparent later conversion to the leftist cause.

The Tamil Tigers was a Tamil group in Sri Lanka that was opposed to the Sinhalese majority and mounted a serious terrorist and guerrilla struggle for more than 25 years before being defeated. It was seeking to create an autonomous homeland or independent Tamil state in the northern and eastern portions of the country.

Theodore Kaczynski was known as the **Unabomber** before he was identified and captured. He sent or placed bombs directed against a variety of targets as part of a protest against modernization and change.

RESOURCES

In the years prior to 2001, the materials on terrorism were relatively limited. There was an occasional book and a handful of edited volumes. There were journal articles but these materials were also few in number. Since 2001 there has been a sometimes bewildering amount of information. The bibliography for this volume, and especially the suggested readings at the end of each chapter, provide a very useful starting point. Of course, there will be more recent materials that have become available. The materials below provide a useful starting point for looking at newer materials as well as the existing information.

BOOKS

There are hundreds of books written about terrorism, most of which focus on terrorism in the years since 9/11. Books prior to that period most frequently deal with terrorism in Europe and Latin America by leftist groups and terrorism by Palestinian groups. Needless to say, most of the materials after 9/11 focus on Islamic groups. Of course, there has always been terrorism by religious groups in all periods, ethnic groups, and other types of ideological groups. The bibliography that follows includes some of the most useful books in the field. More recent works by the same authors are also likely to be very useful. In general, books from academic presses or books from presses that produce textbooks for university courses are likely to contain valid information and well supported conclusions. More popular books include both ones that are extremely worthwhile and others of lesser value.

JOURNAL ARTICLES

Virtually all journals in political science, international relations, and sociology will have articles that deal with some aspect of terrorism. Journals in many other fields deal with aspects of terrorism as well. There are a few academic journals that tend to specialize on terrorism issues. While a list of journals that carry articles on terrorism with some regularly would be quite extensive, there are three that are valuable as starting points: *Terrorism and Political Violence*, *Studies in Conflict and Terrorism*, and *Perspectives on Terrorism*, a recent journal which is also an online journal.

WEBSITES

Websites dealing with terrorism are plentiful as well. Many of them reflect particular ideological perspectives or the views of the persons who create them. They do not necessarily involve any detailed analysis of the issues involved in terrorism. Some of the study centers and or other websites are supported by governments or by groups that receive extensive government support. They tend to reflect the views of the government in power and can be used by the governments. Websites, as a result, need to be accessed with great care. There are many websites that basically provide information on books, articles, and other papers on terrorism. Search engines can be useful as well, although the number of hits that will be generated will be in the hundreds of thousands. Google scholar will provide more precise information based on key terms and avoid some of the less useful materials that deal with terrorism. Addresses for websites can be tricky since they can change from time to time, but search engines can usually provide access to current versions through the name of the group if the website address has changed.

The Jamestown Foundation maintains a website that can serve as a starting point to search out materials on terrorism, and it seeks to avoid any ideological bias in its information (http://www.jamestown.org/programs/gta/terrorismfocusgta).

Most governments maintain websites providing information on terrorism and counterterrorism. The one for the United Kingdom is the Counter Terrorism Portal (http://www.powerbase.info/index.php?title=Counter-Terrorism_Portal). There are similar websites for the United States that are noted below with the data websites. Of course, such government websites need to be used with a bit of care since governments have their own agendas at times.

There are a number of websites that contain useful data on terrorist incidents that can be consulted. The Global Terrorism Database (also known as National Consortium for the Study of Terrorism and Responses to Terrorism or START) is maintained by the University of Maryland. It contains information on incidents from around the world for the years from 1970 to 2008 (with the information being updated through later years). The information can be categorized in a number of ways. The data from 1970 to 1997 are only for international terrorist incidents. The data from 1998 onward are for both international and domestic terrorist incidents (http://www.start.umd.edu/gtd/). This database carries forward and continues the earlier collections of material by the RAND Centre in St. Andrews and then the National Memorial Institute for the Prevention of Terrorism.

The United States National Counterterrorism Center has issued annual reports on terrorism beginning in 2005. The reports which can be accessed electronically provide summary statistics for those years (http://wits-classic.nctc.gov/Reports.do). Earlier years were issued by the Department of State as Patterns of Global Terrorism. Years from 1995 to 2003 are available on an archive page http://www.state.gov/s/ct/rls/index.htm

Worldwide Incidents Tracking System (WITS), National Counterterrorism Center maintains a useful database. This website has incident data for terrorist incidents from 2004 through 2009. It is possible to derive information by target type, country, and other characteristics. It provides opportunities to organize the data in a number of ways (http://wits.nctc.gov/

FederalDiscoverWITS/index.do?t=Reports&Rcv=Facility&Nf=p_
IncidentDate|GTEQ+20090101||p_IncidentDate|LTEQ+200912
31&N=0).

Many universities also have centers that focus on the study of terrorism. Websites for these centers often will have useful information or point people in the right direction in terms of additional materials. Among the better know centers are the Centre for the Study of Terrorism and Political Violence at St. Andrews University in the United Kingdom (http://www.st-andrews.ac.uk/~wwwir/research/cstpv/), the Centre for Terrorism and Counterterrorism Studies (CTC) of Leiden University (The Hague Campus) (http://www.terrorismdata.leiden.edu/), and the Combating Terrorism Center at the US military academy at West Point (http://www.ctc.usma.edu/).

REFERENCES

Abrams, M (2006) "Why Terrorism Does Not Work," *International Security*, 31, 2: 42–78.

Ash, T. G. (2003) "Is There a Good Terrorist," in C. W. Kegley, Jr. (ed.), *The New Global Terrorism: Characteristics, Causes, Controls*. Upper Saddle River, NJ: Prentice Hall, 60–70.

Atran, S. (2008) "Who Becomes a Terrorist Today," *Perspectives on Terrorism*, 2, 5: 3–10.

Badey, T. J. (1998) "Defining International Terrorism: A Pragmatic Approach," *Terrorism and Political Violence*, 10, 1: 90–107.

Banerjee, S. (1984) *India's Simmering Revolution: The Naxalite Uprising*. London: Zed Books.

Banks, W. C., R. de Nevers, and M. B. Wallerstein (2008) *Combating Terrorism: Strategies and Approaches*. Washington DC: CQ Press.

Benjamin, D. and S. Simon (2002) *The Age of Sacred Terror*. New York: Random House.

Bjorgo, T. (1997) *Racist and Right-Wing Violence in Scandinavia: Patterns, Perpetrators, and Responses*. Oslo: Tano Aschehougs.

—— (2005a) "Introduction," in T. Bjorgo (ed.), *Root Causes of Terrorism: Myths, Reality, and Ways Forward*, London: Routledge, 1–15.

——— (ed.) (2005b) *Root Causes of Terrorism: Myths, Reality, and Ways Forward.* London: Routledge.

Cameron, G. (1999) "Multi-Track Microproliferation: Lessons from Aum Shinrikyo and Al Qaeda," *Studies in Conflict and Terrorism*, 22, 4: 277–309.

Campbell, B. D. and A. D. Brenner (eds.), (2000) *Death Squads in Global Perspective: Murder with Deniability*, New York: St. Martin's.

Corsun, A. (1992) "Group Profile: The Revolutionary Organization 17 November in Greece (1975–1991)," in Y. Alexander and D. A. Pluchinsky (eds.), *European Terrorism: Today and Tomorrow*, Washington, DC: Brassey's, 93–125.

Crenshaw, M. (2003) "The Causes of Terrorism," in C. W. Kegley, Jr. (ed.), *The New Global Terrorism: Characteristics, Causes, Controls.* Upper Saddle River, NJ: Prentice Hall, 92–105.

Cronin, A. K. (2009) *How Terrorism Ends: Understanding the Decline and Demise of Terrorist Campaigns.* Princeton, NJ: Princeton University Press.

Dolnik, A. (2008) "13 Years since Tokyo: Re-Visiting the 'Superterrorism' Debate," *Perspectives on Terrorism*, 2, 2: 3–11.

Dolnik, A. and A. Bhattacharjee (2002) "Hamas Suicide Bombings, Rockets, or WMD?" *Terrorism and Political Violence*, 14, 3: 109–28.

Dolnik, A. and R. Gunaratna (2006) "Dagger and Sarin: The Evolution of Terrorist Weapons and Tactics," in A. T. H. Tan (ed.), *The Politics of Terrorism*. London: Routledge, 25–39.

Drake, C. J. M. (1998) "The Role of Ideology in Terrorists' Target Selection," *Terrorism and Political Violence*, 10, 2: 53–85.

Enders, W. and T. Sandler (2000) "Is Transnational Terrorism becoming More Threatening?" *Journal of Conflict Resolution*, 44, 3: 307–302.

——— (2006) *The Political Economy of Terrorism.* New York: Cambridge University Press.

Fair, C. C. (2005) "Diaspora Involvement in Insurgencies: Insights from the Khalistan and Tamil Eelam Movements," *Nationalism and Ethnic Politics*, 11, 1: 125–56.

Hacker, F. J. (1976) *Crusaders, Criminals, and Crazies: Terror and Terrorism in Our Times.* New York: Norton.

Heymann, P. B. (2003) *Terrorism, Freedom, and Security.* Cambridge, MA: MIT Press.

Hoffman, B. (2006) *Inside Terrorism*, revised and expanded edition, New York: Columbia University Press.

Horgan, J. (2003) "The Search for the Terrorist Personality," in A. Silke (ed.), *Terrorists, Victims, and Society: Psychological Perspectives on Terrorism and Its Consequences*. Chichester: Wiley, 3–27.

Horgan, J. and K. Braddock (2010) "Rehabilitating the Terrorists? Challenges in Assessing the Effectiveness of De-Radicalization Programs," *Terrorism and Political Violence*, 22, 2: 267–91.

Jenkins, B. M. (1981) *Embassies under Siege: A Review of 48 Embassy Takeovers, 1971–1980*. Santa Monica, CA: Rand.

Josephus (1981) *The Jewish War*, trans. G. A. Williamson. New York: Dorset Press.

Kaarthikeyan, S. D. R. (2005) "Root Causes of Terrorism? A Case Study of the Tamil Insurgency and the LTTE," in T. Bjorgo (ed.), *Root Causes of Terrorism: Myths, Reality and Ways Forward*. London: Routledge, 131–40.

Kaplan, J. and L. Weinberg (1998) *The Emergence of a Euro-American Radical Right*. New Brunswick, NJ: Rutgers University Press.

Karmon, E. (2002) "Countering NBC Terrorism," in A. Tan and K. Ramakrishna (eds.), *The New Terrorism: Anatomy, Trends and Counter-Strategies*. Singapore: Eastern Universities Press, 101–21.

Korteweg, R., with S. Gohel, F. Heisbourg, M. Ranstorp, and R. de Wijk (2010) "Background Contributing Factors to Terrorism: Radicalization and Recruitment," in M. Ranstorp (ed.), *Understanding Violent Radicalisation: Terrorist and Jihadist Movements in Europe*. London: Routledge, 21–49.

Kuznar, L. A. and J. M. Lutz (2007) "Risk Sensitivity and Terrorism," *Political Studies*, 55, 2: 341–61.

Kydd, A. H., and B. F. Walter (2006) "The Strategies of Terrorism," *International Organization*, 31, 1: 49-80.

Laqueur, W. (1977) *Terrorism*. Boston, MA: Little Brown.

—— (2001) *A History of Terrorism*. New Brunswick, NJ: Transaction Publishers.

Leiken, R. S. (2005) "Europe's Angry Muslims," *Foreign Affairs*, 84, 4: 120–35.

Lutz, J. M. and B. J. Lutz (2006) "Terrorism as Economic Warfare," *Global Economy Journal*, 6, 2: 1–20.

—— (2008) *Global Terrorism*, 2nd edn, London: Routledge.

—— (2009) "How Successful Is Terrorism?" Forum on Public Policy, http:// forumonpublicpolicy.com/spring09papers/papers09spring.html, 1–22.

Maleckova, J. (2005) "Impoverished Terrorists: Stereotypes or Reality," in T. Bjorgo (ed.), *Root Causes of Terrorism: Myths, Reality, and Ways Forward*. London: Routledge, 33–43.

Michael, G. (2003) *Confronting Right-Wing Extremism and Terrorism in the USA*. New York: Routledge.

O'Neil, A. (2003) "Terrorist Use of Weapons of Mass Destruction: How Serious Is the Threat?" *Australian Journal of International Affairs*, 57, 1: 99–112.

Pape, R. A (2005) *Dying to Win: The Logic of Suicide Terrorism*. New York: Random House.

Pillar, P. R. (2001) *Terrorism and U.S. Foreign Policy*. Washington DC: Brookings Institution.

Piszkiewicz, D. (2003) *Terrorism's War with America: A History*. Westport, CT: Praeger.

Raphaeli, N. (2003) "Financing of Terrorism: Sources, Methods, and Channels," *Terrorism and Political Violence*, 15, 4: 59–82.

Richardson, L. (ed.) (2006) *The Roots of Terrorism*. London: Routledge.

Robbins, J. S. (2002) "Bin Laden's War," in R. D. Howard and R. L. Sawyer (eds.), *Terrorism and Counterterrorism: Understanding the New Security Environment, Readings and Interpretations*, Guildford, CT: McGraw-Hill/ Duskin, 354–66.

Rodell, P. A. (2007) "Separatist Insurgency in the Southern Philippines," in A. T. H. Tan (ed.), *A Handbook of Terrorism and Insurgency in Southeast Asia*. Cheltenham: Edward Elgar, 225–47.

Schmid, A. P. (1992) "The Response Problem as a Definition Problem," *Terrorism and Political Violence*, 4, 4: 7–13.

Sederberg, P. C. (2003) "Global Terrorism: Problems of Challenge and Response," in in C. W. Kegley, Jr. (ed.), *The New Global Terrorism: Characteristics, Causes, Controls*. Upper Saddle River, NJ: Prentice Hall, 267–84.

Silke, A. (2004) "An Introduction to Terrorism Research," in A. Silke (ed.), *Research on Terrorism: Trends, Achievements and Failures*. London: Frank Cass, 1–29.

——(2005) "Fire of Iolaus: The Role of State Countermeasures in Causing Terrorism and What Needs to be Done," in T. Bjorgo (ed.), *Root Causes of Terrorism: Myths, Reality, and Ways Forward*. London: Routledge, 241–55.

Sproat, P. A. (1991) "Can the State Be Terrorist," *Terrorism*, 14, 1: 19–29.

Stern, J. (2000) "Pakistan's Jihad Culture," *Foreign Affairs*, 79, 6: 115–26.

Stern, J. and M. Modi (2008) "Producing Terror: Organizational Dynamics of Survival," in T. J. Biersteker and S. E. Eckert (eds.), *Countering the Financing of Terrorism*. London: Routledge, 19–46.

Tan, A. H. T. (2000) "Armed Muslim Separatist Rebellion in Southeast Asia: Persistence, Prospects, and Implications," *Studies in Conflict and Terrorism*, 23, 4: 267–88.

—— (2006) *The Politics of Terrorism: A Survey*. London: Routledge.

Tucker, J. B. (ed.), (2000) *Toxic Terror: Use of Chemical and Biological Weapons*. Cambridge, MA: MIT Press.

Wilkinson, P. (1975) *Political Terrorism*. New York: Halstead Press.

—— (2003) "Why Modern Terrorism? Differentiating Types and Distinguishing Ideological Motivations," in C. W. Kegley, Jr. (ed.), *The New Global Terrorism: Characteristics, Causes, Controls*. Upper Saddle River, NJ: Prentice Hall, 106–38.

Williams, P. (2008) "Terrorist Financing and Organized Crime: Nexus, Appropriation, or Transformation?" in T. J. Biersteker and S. E. Eckert (eds.), *Countering the Financing of Terrorism*. London: Routledge, 126–49.

INDEX